LIVING FORWARD

LIVING FORWARD

Perspectives on reaching "a certain age"

John F. Smith

SORIN BOOKS   Notre Dame, Indiana

www.sorinbooks.com

International Standard Book Number: 1-893732-58-4

Cover design by Dave Scholtes

Text design by Katherine Robinson Coleman

Printed and bound in the United States of America

Library of Congress Cataloging-in-Publication Data
Smith, John Ferris.
Living forward : perspectives on reaching "a certain age" / John F. Smith.
    p. cm.
  ISBN 1-893732-58-4 (pbk.)
  1. Retirement--Psychological aspects. 2. Self-actualization (Psychology) 3. Maturation (Psychology) 4. Retirement--Religious aspects--Christianity. 5. Retirees--Conduct of life. I. Title.
HQ1062 S613 2003
306.3'8--dc21
                                       2002013325
                                            CIP

THIS BOOK IS DEDICATED

TO MY GRANDCHILDREN,

SAM, LUCY, AND VANESSA

CONTENTS

INTRODUCTION

A lady of a "certain age," which means, Certainly
aged.

BYRON, *DON JUAN*

A wise rabbi says, "God loves the truth."
If we turn the light of that remark on
ourselves we come to realize that means
that God loves the truth of ourselves,
the plain truth of who we are. God is always at us to
discover our truth. It's not letting down the integrity
of God to say that the truth of ourselves changes, that
is, we discover new truths about ourselves as we grow
older. They are deeper, stronger truths, and God loves
that deeper truth. We may find ourselves a little
tougher than before, having grown stronger as we
aged, able to face some of the truths revealed in what
we've done and been—good truths and hard truths,

lovely beautiful truths and unpleasant truths—tough enough to bear and face the truth.

One of the gifts of our time of life, for those of us who are of a "certain age"—that is, the young-old, those facing retirement, retired, or refusing to retire—is that we haven't gotten fuzzy or soft. We've gotten tougher, more able to face ourselves, more able to feel with people, more, we hope, compassionate because of where we've been and what we've been. We know who we are; it is our truth. We have no need to deny the truth about ourselves, because God loves the truth; if it's good enough for God, it's good enough for us.

This book is about the truth of aging that God apparently wants us to face. We have reached "a certain age," the time when one look at us tells people where we are in life, on the threshold of old age. We are vigorous, eligible for a "senior" ticket at the movies, engaged in life, and physically able, though perhaps not for competitive snowboarding (we wouldn't want to wear those clothes anyway), although some will consider it. However, we do ski, run, play golf and tennis, swim, lift weights, occasionally drive our cars too fast. We will not pull all-nighters, but we work hard and we are ready to dance the night away once in a while. We are capable of working hard because we work smarter. So there is time for us, either now or in the near future, to ponder, consider the great questions, questions of the meaning and purpose of life: Where did I come from? Where am I going? What did I learn? Who am I? What is my truth? What is my truth of God? These are the nagging, good questions of any time of life; we are now able to face them in a truly mature way.

It's too bad that it's most often during late adolescence and early adulthood when people are asked to consider the great questions, led to it either by the wide river of life that stretches before us or forced to do so by a required class in philosophy or religion. Now, there are no requirements binding us, and we fulfilled the prerequisites for this study long ago. We are, not to exaggerate, tempered by the fires of life. We have met the enemy, know that he is us, and we have recognized our face in the face of the world. We are facing at least fifteen years (the average life span after retirement) of the possibility of vigorous engagement in the world, either working or performing its equivalent in volunteer and other activities. We are built for comfort, not for speed, but comfort for us does not mean losing our edge; it means taking our time, it means, in the old and deep sense of the word, being strengthened. We may be a step behind, but not two steps.

We have an enormous advantage: we have learned from our children, and/or from the young people whom we brought along, a great deal about how to face people and issues. We have rejoiced with them, mourned with them, loved their energy, their goodness, their stupidity, and this has changed us too, to see ourselves in them from the outside.

So this is the time to do some thinking, to take those walks, sail that boat, stand in that river, read those books, write those poems, play that music, build that furniture, listen to those young people. It's time to reflect, drawing on the history of accumulated experience and relationship, on the story of our lives so far. What meaning can philosophical texts have for young people who cannot test them with life experience? While they have meaning in hope, in commitment, in ordering thought, and in direction, those of us who have come to a certain chronological place have the truth of our life to set over against the truth of abstraction. Relatively few things are solely abstract for us. We have seen, if not all, most of it: life and death, young promise extinguished in accident or alcohol, the mistake of marriage, the beauty and wonder of marriage, the foolishness of love, the pain of betrayal, the anguish of failure, the elation of success. Our bags are packed with our past, and, thank you, no, we will not be checking them, they are our carryons forever.

Here are my reflections on some of the issues that have plagued, delighted, puzzled, worried, and elated me. I cannot promise you to stay by your side all along the way. Like you I will be jumping up to go to meetings, to get other work done, to exercise, to check in with my grandchildren, to correspond with the young people who've been important in my life, sometimes just walking away from my desk because I can do it—to see a movie, play some music, read a book, walk the dog, have dinner with friends, take a trip. The search for my truth about God and my life, and your search for your truth, is neither a direct nor swift journey; we are built for comfort, not for speed, not that some of what we are talking about will make us feel all that comfortable.

Here is your task. I will speak as truthfully as I can about myself, and you must reflect as truthfully as you can about yourself. You may have found paths which wander far from this somewhat cloistered Cape Cod life of mine; it could hardly be otherwise. You may decide that I have gone too far afield, strode into briars and thorns through which it would be foolish for you to walk. Or you may find that I am overly tentative, uncertain, a little mousy. This is your chance to do what you know you've always wanted to do, to figure out some important things for yourself.

You may find that the great questions make their appearance in the guise of small questions. What do I have to give today? What will I learn today? I hope you will learn to love your truth as much as God does, to see your life as leading to your truth, even to a truth which may contradict some parts of your life. We are lucky to have made it to this point in our lives, a time to work hard in another way, to discover and to rediscover our truth.

1

A New Springtime:

Finding Ourselves

Again

I n one of her books, the mystery writer P. D. James writes, "However long we live, there are never enough springs." When we were young, spring brought with it the promise of release from school, maybe a trip to a vacation house, the pleasure of swimming, not wearing a coat, the adventure of camping, the excitement and challenge of baseball or tennis, long, hot hours with a book or with friends endlessly talking, a summer job, driving fairly aimlessly around a town, and, in later years, the bittersweet dance of relationship. The days stretched on into the long evenings; there were games in the street, dances and concerts out of doors. There is a brightness and a length to youthful spring and summer which is undeniable; time moves glacially for the young.

Those of us who are a certain age know spring as excitement tempered with poignancy. We are at least unconsciously aware that there will never be enough springs; spring goes as fast or faster than summer which rushes on to fall. Our lives speed up just as we begin to explore them thoroughly. So spring is regret as well as anticipation, regret that springs before were not sufficiently appreciated, plumbed, and explored, and awareness of the limited number of springs left to us. The twists and turns of life have given us the wisdom that there will never be enough springs, and that we will probably never live them with the intensity they deserve.

And yet, spring and self-knowledge signal opportunity. There is the possibility of renewing ourselves, discovering ourselves all over again, perhaps not so much by physical challenge as by discovering ourselves through a personal spiritual renewal. Just as we oil up our bike or buy a new pair of walking shoes, we prepare to ask ourselves again, with the artist Paul Gauguin, "Where have we been? What are we? Where are we going?" There is an urgency to our renewal because there will never be enough opportunities to rediscover the self, never enough springs.

I remember my father teaching himself to play golf when he retired. Since he was a natural athlete, it was easy for him to do. But it also meant a redefinition of himself as one who had come to a place where participating in this sport was an emotional as well as a physical possibility. In his mind, I think, retirement meant he was a man of leisure and therefore it was appropriate to take up one of the activities of a man of leisure. Playing golf indicated he had rethought who he was, reinvented himself, as it were.

In my retirement, I have recovered my high school clarinet playing, joining a local town band, something of a tradition on Cape Cod. While a few very tolerant younger people of high school and college age join us occasionally, most band members are either approaching, or have achieved, geezerhood. There are wrinkles galore above the various mouthpieces, frowning over the percussion. On the other hand, our band is well known for its spirit; we cheer our audiences, our soloists, our selves, at every opportunity. We are a lively and feisty crowd.

The other day, as we sat on a flatbed truck waiting for a parade to begin (March? Us? Are you kidding?), the Boston College marching band, full of zip, energy, and high spirits, rattled past us, their marching step a kind of dance, shaking their shoulders, bending at the waist, twirling their instruments. We watched with amused appreciation. When they stopped near us, one of our saxophone players, a woman whose formidable life experience is written all over her face, got to her feet and called, "Have a good time. When you're our age you'll be riding on a truck!" The college kids roared with laughter and we laughed back.

If perhaps we ride on a truck and are not quite as fast as some to hear a missed accidental, we are also not bothered when it is pointed out; we have learned to tolerate even ourselves. In our snappy polo shirts and baseball caps with a Cape Cod embroidered on the front, we pop up everywhere we're invited and make a joyful noise. Indeed there are those who wonder if some band members don't occasionally get out of hand. One of my friends attended a concert in our town and afterward shook her head saying, "That's the last time I'll sit that close to the cymbal player!" I had watched earlier the cymbal player warming up. She is a woman of remarkable upper arms and she loosened them up expertly, stretching carefully before taking several practice crashes to get herself in shape. The sound was satisfactorily prodigious, and the discreet listener is wise to take a position somewhat removed, especially during "Stars and Stripes Forever."

The man who sits next to me points out that he came into ownership of his clarinet in 1942, one of our trombonists played with Louis Prima and Artie Shaw, and several other musicians had substantial careers. We were joined for a few weeks by a quiet, self-effacing, modest trumpeter who had played in the Cleveland Orchestra under George Szell and in the Boston Pops. Our trumpet section sat up a little straighter when he was around. We have a lot of experience in a lot of ways.

Most of us are high school and college players getting back a part of ourselves put on hold while we went about the practical business of making a living. We are using retirement and young-old age to recover ourselves, at the same time losing ourselves in the kind of creativity which is not rewarded in our society. Playing in the band is a way of living another spring, recovering, renewing ourselves, knowing ourselves in another way all over again.

Not such a bad idea, to use retirement, any pause in our lives, to discover parts of the self which have been lost, to find ourselves again, to redevelop as a mature person. There are lessons to be learned in the process, much to be relearned, and a number of things to be unlearned. My children and friends are a little stunned at my playing again after so many years. "I never knew you could do that." There are springs to be lived at any time of year, any time of life. We return to the God of the spring who leads us to discover ourselves again, as the springtimes of our youth were times of first discovery. In my teaching career I always looked forward to my students' finding themselves in the spring and summer before their senior year. The discoveries, changes, and maturation of that period were always the most interesting and pleasing.

The other day I was reading a clarinet website discussion on the topic of "How to Practice." I suspect most non-musicians think practicing is a pretty obvious activity. You get out your music and play through it. But what constitutes a good practice period is not at all obvious to those who must do it. There is a long, sometimes acrimonious, debate among clarinetists about whether one is best off practicing long tones or scales, and what proportion of each should be included in the practice period. There is an argument over what constitutes valuable practice. How long one should be at the music stand is a matter of dispute.

What's wrong, one person asks, with a six-hour practice time? (That's an easy question for me!) We amateurs listen carefully to the professionals to figure out what we can apply to our far less demanding musical lives, but it's clear there's much to be learned even about the most mundane activities. One clarinetist pointed out that she played several "studies," or "methods," before she practiced, in order, as it were, to get in practice for practice.

Think of Larry Bird, the famous Boston Celtics basketball player. Every day Bird would throw at least one hundred and fifty baskets, even when he was playing at the very top of his game. That's how he practiced. And that's how musicians practice too. They prepare to practice by practicing scales and exercises and then play over and over again the passages they will need to navigate when they perform; it takes hour after hour. When I play every summer with some professional musicians, our leader is likely to say, after we have spent a long time working a couple of measures into shape, "Let's just play it five more times."

When I was reminded of the "method" approach of practicing, I looked in my own old student book and found the very method espoused by one of the clarinetists on the website. These pieces are termed by insiders the "Rose Etudes." I play several of them not very well each day, and at my age find very satisfying and helpful something at which I would have groaned at as a not very dedicated (in the sense of working hard) clarinetist at age sixteen. I discovered on the somewhat yellowed pages the dates on which my old teacher had indicated these practice studies were due,

4/29/49, 10/16/50, etc. Every day I struggle with a few of them, attempting to bring back muscle memory, hand-eye coordination, and "lip" to the point they were when I was a teenager.

There aren't enough springs, I suspect, to get this all done, but I have the advantage these days of another kind of time, a little more patience, and some wisdom about myself gained from struggling with all sorts of challenges. I am aware that I am not that sixteen-year-old, vastly more aware now of my self, my limitations, my likely stumbles, my possibilities. I know that, for example, I am likely to play the study moderately well the first time, and fumble over and over on the next few tries. I'm a quick study, but then anxiety takes over; it's been true all my life. But at least much of the teenage angst is gone, replaced by a more refined elderly version. I realize that on a larger stage, all my life has been a kind of practice, sometimes fitful, sometimes superficial, sometimes on the mark, for life lived now in retirement. "How long did it take you to write that sermon?" "All my life." The same thing is true for the now time of retirement. On the other hand, there is a way in which practicing is not just preparation but the thing itself, just as in *King Lear*. Shakespeare refers to the "poor, bare, forked animal" of humanity as "the thing itself." It's not as if the performance is real and the practice something lesser. It's all "the thing itself."

Taking advantage of the springs we have left and the renewal they offer brings wisdom, knowledge of the self before God. This wisdom, a depth of self-knowledge and the limits of knowledge and the self, is sensed rather than known in the usual way. It can't be told; it can only be lived. We communicate to ourselves and to those around us knowledge of ourselves, along with our respect for and wonder about life, our never-dying hope, our trust that God has made worthwhile so much in the world, and our faith that those revelations will continue to come. We continue to work, like a clarinetist practicing scales, toward a knowledge of ourselves which is deep and hidden, a more profound appreciation of the mystery of the world and of our relationship to God.

Along the way we find ourselves interesting, not in a self-centered and narcissistic way, but in a way which aligns knowledge of the self as a created being with knowledge of the self as known by God. We are willing to follow whatever leads we can toward that discovery. For some the path to wisdom will be music; for others, sports, like my father; for others volunteering at local social service agencies or schools, or helping local entrepreneurs found new businesses. In these activities, as older people, we are carrying on the human work of self-discovery, a sacred task, one our grandchildren are aware of. We seek to know ourselves as God knows us.

Thoughtful people encounter God in different ways at different times, always unique, yet the same One in relation. We have recognized God as showing herself in different ways in different times, but still as the only God who is God. The God we have met in various religious contexts is sometimes the first God we leave behind as we are in process to what we hope is a

deeper, more fully realized relationship. The God who
is a God of the living, not of the dead, however,
remains elusive. We are not in control of God; he is
not us, she is not the projection of our dreams and
hopes, not the bearer of our prejudices and inclina-
tions. God remains a gracious resource, deeply hidden,
acting in us in God's own way, not in ours, revealing
God's own self in ways which require thought, dis-
cernment, silence, acceptance.

And yet God remains, the God who expects us to be
ourselves before him, a God who exists in us as we
come to trust her. Knowing God as unknown and
known is an important insight, one which makes us
valuable people in the lives of those around us. We
who have grown up with and in God are satisfied with
"seeming" because we know God destroying as well as
building up, in the sense that one destroys when he
digs up the garden to prepare it for the new season.
God is always preparing us for deeper, more profound
insights and knowledge, knowledge of the self and of
the world.

We are always building anew with God, not trapped in
the certainty of human conceptions, building in the
midst of tearing down. Such complexity, such a
nuanced understanding of God, is ours as we grow
into the God of the living. Those whose lives have
been touched by the living God will never condemn
without questioning, never accept without question or
consideration. We are too old for that; we have
experienced too much. We know that what once was
certain is now uncertain, but that very uncertainty has

power, authenticity, and graciousness. In our own way we have practiced very hard all our lives, concentrated, worked through it, and this conversation of certainty and uncertainty is something with which we are comfortable and familiar. Our practice has become our life, and God is in all of it.

Dame Julian of Norwich, living in her little anchorite (hermit) cell in fourteenth-century England, held a small nut, a filbert or hazelnut, in her hand and saw in it all the world, all the creation, the knowing and the unknowing. Her message from God was ". . . all manner of things shall be well." We know in her the "vanity and futility of seeking perfection," living with the uncertainty of God while knowing that in ways beyond knowing, all things shall be well.

The point of all this pondering is, ironically enough, us. There are ways in which all that we know about God is ourselves. I know that sounds egocentric in a tradition which has always been aware of the dangers of regarding the human self as the center of the universe. But, whether we like it or not, God's project, successful or not, seems to be us. For some reason God seems to be interested less in himself than in humanity and in the creation.

At least one of the challenges God presents to us is to accept and love ourselves as God loves us, unconditionally. Instinctively those of us in the older generation shrink from what we regard not only as vain, but also as soft, leading to smugness, quietism, and self-centered satisfaction with things as they are. We are people of productivity and commitment, hard workers. We have earned what we have and who we are. But we aren't talking now about our physical life in the world. Perhaps this is the time for recognizing a kind of reality which is hard for some of us to accept. We need humility to accept the fact that God cares for us and cares for us as ourselves, as the people we are, with warts and wrinkles, and also as people still struggling to be, that is, as a people of practicing. God's unconditional acceptance of us is sometimes baffling, going counter to our notions of being "self-made," but when we are quiet, lower our resistances, listen deeply to the voice speaking from our imagination, when, finally, we get off our own backs, we know ourselves to be deeply, finally loved. And then, maybe, in response we can love and accept ourselves. This loving care and acceptance of ourselves is a gift; it is our quiet confidence.

We have lived our lives inhabiting various roles: the loyal member of the congregation, the macho man, the widow woman, the faithful priest, the devoted mother, the dutiful daughter, the self-made man, the scorned woman, the family provider, the queen of disapproval, the scarred man of experience, the hard-bitten entrepreneur. I should pause to note that these are not necessarily superficial roles. They are authentic parts of our lives. That is, there are people who are dutiful, scarred, scorned, etc. But it has also been true that part of us has been too busy, too distracted, too consumed to discover our own selves underneath the social roles, and we have put them on like costumes to get us through the turmoil and tumult of life. We have put off the work of self-discovery, often out of necessity, and "prepared a face to meet the faces you meet."

Now at a certain age we have an opportunity to deepen ourselves, to discover another kind of freedom, and another life task. It is to set the roles aside and discover the self we are in our deepest places, our self as known by God, even if not by ourselves. Our children and the younger people who share life with us, who are also in the process of discovering a self, are our companions, fellow travelers, pilgrims, along the road to self. They can be a resource as we engage in conversation with them, the hidden question of which is: what did you find out about yourself today?

> We shall not cease from exploration
> And the end of all our exploring
> Will be to arrive where we started
> And know the place for the first time.
>
> T. S. ELIOT, *FOUR QUARTETS*, V

All this leads us to a question. Who are we before God? We are not actors in some drama dreamed up by others, not playing roles set for us by the hidden powers of this world, but ourselves. At the end of our life, who are we compared to who we were when we were our grandchildren's age; what of then remains in us? Who are we now in ourselves?

And therefore, what is our wisdom? What do we truly know about ourselves as known by God? What better spiritual inheritance can we leave except the knowledge

of our being known by God? This is my spiritual legacy, the person I am, for better or worse.

So we are called again to travel a path. We could rein-
terpret the familiar reading in which Jesus speaks to
Peter ". . . when you were younger, you used to fasten
your belt and go wherever you wished. But when you
grow old, you will stretch out your hands, and someone else will fasten a belt around you and take you
where you do not wish to go." There comes a time
when we are led to discover parts of ourselves that pre-
viously we were too young or too weak to understand.
The strength of age allows us to face ourselves in honest ways that would have been impossible earlier; it
allows us, even forces us, to confront ourselves before
God, perhaps to discover things we do not wish to
know, to go places we did not wish to go. We walk this
path with God who has been with us all the while but
now leads us through the valley to the still waters of
ourselves. This is what we know of God as we walk the
journey of our life through our springs, that we are
known endlessly, thoroughly, forever.

2

TAKING A
TRIP
AND
FINDING
OURSELVES

People of a certain age who wish to live a healthy and reasonably happy life are accustomed to living forward, to seeing the possibilities and openness of the road which lies ahead. However, if we want to live a deep and fulfilled older age, it is important also to look back, to see the path over which we have come. What experiences have turned us, twisted us, perhaps pounded us into a certain shape?

Some of us remember the song in which a woman sings, "You made me what I am today; I hope you're satisfied." We look back without that bitterness, with only a few regrets, but we still look back in order to understand. We have no need to live in the past, but it's important to visit the past in order to get a perspective on the present. And it's all about the remarkable trip we've taken through our lives.

A quotation from the German theologian Dietrich Bonhoeffer hangs beside the kitchen door in my house: "There is a meaning in every journey which is unknown to the traveler." This line is especially poignant in light of Bonhoeffer's journey to his death; a resister to Hitler, he was killed on April 9, 1945, at Flossenburg concentration camp. But it is also a line which informs much of what I have done and been over the past forty-odd years of my working life as a college and boarding school chaplain, though certainly not with the seriousness and profundity of Dietrich Bonhoeffer. As I approach my seventieth year I have reached a stage on this obscure journey when it is time to look back, inquire about meanings, and attempt to articulate some of them. For me it has been an odd, rough journey with God, all which seems to be God's choice, not stumbling, confused mine. It is time to interrogate that journey as it begins to approach the end, the late autumn of life, and to reflect on what have I learned about God, who seems now to me to have been the meaning of my life.

So here I pass on what it has been like to have been known by God. The relatively short physical journey I have taken, from Detroit to Boston to Groton (a small town northwest of Boston) to Cape Cod where I now live in retirement, had a spiritual meaning which is gradually being revealed, all in good time. There was an interior journey parallel to the physical journey during which I discovered something about myself and thereby learned something about God, the God who seems to be present with me in the places I've been, in the factory town of my birth, in college, at the urban university where I was chaplain, and at the elite boarding school where I ended my work-life; God with me, known and unknown, opening doors to another understanding, leading onward. These were often understandings which I resisted, questioned (which was right), finally accepted, walking backward, as one poet says. Like most people I am resistant to self-knowledge and notoriously resistant to facing what is, as my mother would say, as plain as the nose on your face.

My journey with God is not so much different, I'm convinced, from the spiritual journeys of many of us who were born, raised, and worked through the tumultuous past sixty-odd years. I am no pioneer, no adventurer, no hero of faith, just as most of God's people have not been heroes, or saints; we are the holy common people of God which, by the way, seems to suit God just fine.

It is partially because I am convinced that I have traveled this way with so many people that I have decided to write about it, to speak as one like the dead man who in one of the Christian gospels came out of the grave "hands and feet bound with strips of cloth and face wrapped in a cloth," to hear the order given, "Unbind him, and let him go."

The metaphor of journey, from blindness to sight, makes clear that the goal of knowing God is unfinished, has yet more stages, the meanings of which are unknown to me, but surely known to God, just as in so many ways I remain unknown to myself, yet known to God.

There are a number of things to say, though I am not sure of the exact way to say them, as I also can never be sure of their absolute meanings. This is because meaning is up to God, the God who seems disinterested in himself, concerned and interested in human beings (so unlike us, one might add), disinterested in religion, as Archbishop Temple noted, and wrapped up in human history and human life. It would be easier if we were convinced that God did not care, was not present, did not journey with his people through the wilderness, toward, we hope, the promised land of milk and honey. The God we know is engaged with her people, ordinary people, people who struggle from one job to another, who raise families, fail, stumble, turn into blind corners because they close their eyes, refuse to see the truth, people who bring meaning to others of which they were unaware, who work hard, doubt, believe, love, and occasionally, alas, hate. I'm talking about myself.

There were two moments among many which I recall as being turning points in my understanding, though I certainly did not know their meaning at the time. I choose them almost randomly. In the middle sixties I went with a group to meet with staff at the Navy Chaplains' Training School at Newport, Rhode Island. We were a group of people who supposedly knew "young adults" and what they were up to; the Navy was considering hiring us as consultants. As part of an orientation briefing which would help us to understand what the chaplains were up against, we were asked to wander about Newport on a weekend night. There, we were told we would see the true pathos of the lives of the younger sailors.

So a group of us went out that night into Newport and wandered up and down, stopping into a bar for a beer, looking around, trying to get a sense of what we'd been told were the desperate, lonely, spiritually empty young people who were sailors. When we got back to where we were staying we sat around for a while and talked about what we had seen. It seemed to me that what we'd seen was a bunch of kids out on the town, having a fairly good time. I'm sure there would be the occasional fight and the usual stupid, stumbling drunk, but we stayed out quite late and saw little of that. In my usual, subtle, slick way (I'm speaking ironically) I suggested that perhaps those who could only see young people who were alienated, desperate, and seeking oblivion might just be projecting some of their own feelings on the sailors. This was not received very positively. Needless to say our group did not get a contract to consult with the Navy chaplains. We had not seen the right things. Or had we?

What we saw were happy, reasonably satisfied, lively young people jumping into a good time on a night off. It is certainly conceivable that some of them were in the midst of a spiritual crisis, but it was more conceivable that most of them were well-integrated, decent, together people. Of course you could say that underneath (where only the professionally religious can see) the sailors lacked depth, were not settled, were alienated, wandering, etc., but you *could* have said that about the chaplains, and the visiting consultants.

Years later I read Thomas Merton, the great American spiritual writer, who told about going one day on a trip to Louisville from his monastery. He hadn't been in a city for many years, having sought monastic life as a refuge from a world which he believed to be utterly corrupt and without hope. He wrote about that journey later in a letter and described how as he stood on a corner and looked around him: " . . . I got the feeling that everybody was of terrific value, immensely precious and bought with a great price and all their souls were like jewels, very rich. . . ." That trip, and that view of human beings, marked a turning point in Merton's life. He literally turned a corner in his appreciation of people and life in the world and God's abiding presence. Merton was enabled in that moment to see the glory of God in the face of humanity, and that insight challenged him for the rest of his life.

In the same way, the trip to Newport marked a kind of turning point for me, though I did not know it at the time, a time when I began to suspect that the lives of people were not as desperate, hopeless, and empty as many religious people liked to think. The young people were not despairing; God had, in fact, not left them to the beast, but was alive and active, calling them to life, reflection, and thought. There is, in fact, a kind of unconquerable joy in the world.

Because the Holy Ghost over the bent
World broods with warm breast and with ah!
    bright wings.

G. M. HOPKINS, "GOD'S GRANDEUR"

God is present to all people, whether the professionally religious like it or not, present even in places where
it might be thought it would be unwise, or unprofes-
sional, for God to be. God may be more comfortable
with those who are considered to be his enemies than
those thought to be his friends.

So there's been a tendency for me to look less at
human alienation and more for the presence of God,
healing, reconciling, encouraging, filling the world
with joy. I hope you won't think I've been going
around with a silly grin on my face, ignoring the signs
of suffering, violence, separation, and alienation
which are obviously present in the world—the presence of unearned, unacknowledged privilege for
whites, males, straight people; the devilish notion that
problems can be solved by violence. The fact that I'm
white and male is apparent to me not only physically
but mentally and spiritually. But there is "the dearest
freshness deep down things," and people of faith have
a responsibility to affirm that in the midst of the ugli-
ness and evil of the world. I'm sure there was an
undercurrent to life on the streets of Newport which
was neither pleasant nor life-giving, as there is everywhere—on Rodeo Drive, in Greenwich, in
Disneyland—but there were also happy, bumptious
sailors having a good time with friends, and there was
no particular need for them all to be discussing

Thomas Mann, C. S. Lewis, or Aloysius Gonzaga on the odd Saturday night in Newport.

The other turning point for me, one which I thought at the time was merely an offhand theological quip, occurred at the end of a day of meetings at a conference. Several of us went out to have a beer with a professor at Harvard Divinity School (later dean of that institution and still later presiding bishop of the Swedish Lutheran Church). The conversation turned to young people and to sex. It was the middle sixties— we talked a lot about sex. The professor remarked on how easy it was to get young people, unformed and vulnerable as they were, to feel guilty about sex. And then, he pointed out, how easy it was to relieve them of the guilt through forgiveness and thus earn their gratitude. He noted that the cheapest kind of religion in the world manipulated people into guilt and then forgave them as a method of recruitment, easing them into dependency. I am sure that I am not remembering the elegance and subtlety of his thought (and he is not responsible for what I took away from an innocent remark), but this was his conversation as I remember it, especially the part about eliciting guilt, relieving it, and developing dependence on religious institutions.

This is the great religious temptation, one into which it is so easy to fall, another way of tying and binding people rather than relieving them of the bonds of social and religious convention and freeing them to be themselves before God. I believe that our connections with synagogue, mosque, church, and temple should be as freely chosen as possible, and that God is all about humanization, the freedom of men and women who respond to God's presence in commitments to society and communities in society, people who are called to the common good.

These two moments, in Newport and with the Harvard professor, were moments about which I did not know the meaning at the time, but they have unconsciously, I'm sure, informed my living and my thinking. "Unbind him and let him go."

One comes to these reflections after some time; they seep into your consciousness, occasionally bursting into light. One has experiences like the above, one takes a trip and things happen, a story develops, but the meaning of the story remains to be revealed. Sometimes it grows from the edges, not from the middle.

Toward the end of her life my mother suffered from macular degeneration, a condition of the retina which leads to blindness, a peculiar symptom of which is that one sees more clearly on the periphery, that is, out of the corner of the eyes, than straight ahead. There were those who said my mother was always more interested in the corners than in what was plain and clear, and perhaps I am somewhat like her. The odd and quirky, what lies beneath, insight, and the unsuspected value seem to interest me. This is where I have met the God who exists everywhere, but everywhere hidden, anonymous.

I remember a young student at school who could never seem to keep his shirt tucked in. He was a delightful, smart boy who was not in any way particularly rebellious. However, whenever you saw him the shirt was always out so that those teaching colleagues who believed—not obsessively but reasonably—that the dress code, simple as it was, meant generally that students should be neat and clean, got tired of reminding the boy I'll call Matt about it. "Maybe just once a day," someone suggested. It got to be a game to see how long Matt would last tucked in. I remember noticing at one chapel service that he started the service looking fine but when he shook my hand at the door an hour later his shirt was drooping below his blazer. There couldn't have been that much physical activity in church to pull it out. Our services did not involve a lot of leaping about. It was just the way he was.

I think now there was something sweet and sacred about Matt's untucked shirt, some bumpy rhythm in him, some impulse that will never stay tucked in. There are those tendencies in all of us, those interior pushes which are not only sweet but also sacred, which come from depths all unknown. We notice them from the corners of our eyes, which are unbound enough to see through appearances to the reality which lies below. It seems to me that I have learned about God in that way, in reflecting on the weird and the barely noticeable, seen out of the corners of our eyes, but indisputably there. Gertrude Stein said, referring to Oakland, California, "There's no there there." But I am referring to events, moments, incidents in which there is definitely a "there," even though we're not sure of the tenor and quality of "there" at the time.

Right now I am reflecting on the experience of a lifetime with God, reporting on what I have learned and what I wish to leave to others as a kind of legacy. It will not be your experience, but it will inform your experience, seep into the walls of your consciousness, break down and build up. Maybe you would reflect yourself on what have been the turning points in your spiritual life—wrong turnings as well as life-giving moments. I offer mine to you as a gift, as so much has been offered me as a gift from those who surrounded me: the mother who saw out of the corner of her eyes, the sailors in Newport, the distinguished biblical scholar, the boy who could not keep his shirt tucked in.

3

SAYING GOODBYE

TO

CHILDHOOD GODS

Thoughtful people encounter God in different ways at different times. Those of us who are of a certain age have grown through various phases of personal spirituality, while not being able to give up spirituality. Some of the gods we have worshiped have been put away as not worthy of God—childish gods, gods of ethnic and cultural narrowness, gods of the past, of the dead, not of the living. Other times we have recognized God revealing herself in different ways in different times, still the only God who is God, the God of justice and peace, the God who loves our truth, even our stumbling truths about God.

We have often been disappointed by religious institutions. Many people today are deeply disturbed by the seeming indifference of clergy and the institution to the sexual abuse of children; others are bothered by the way religious institutions adjust themselves comfortably to the prevailing culture rather than confronting it.

In any case, the God we have sometimes met in various religious contexts, as children perhaps, is the first God who goes, no matter what disturbance this might cause. Our truth is that we needed to get rid of that childhood God as we are in process to what we hope is a deeper relationship with God, a relationship suitable to a person with our experience and age. God, however, remains elusive and anonymous. We are not in control of God; he is not us, she is not the projection of our dreams and hopes. God remains a gracious resource, deeply hidden, anonymous. The truth is that God is less interested in God than in us and in those who share life with us.

I was talking a few weeks ago with a friend who has written beautifully and profoundly about the Holocaust. As we shared coffee he spoke of Auschwitz, the death camp, as an "abyss of meaning," meaning that it made so little sense, was so absurd, was such an outrage to humanity on every level, that one had best refuse even to try to make sense of it, to allow that horror its full depth of meaninglessness and emptiness, a destruction of destructions, an abomination of desolation—language used to describe the pollution of the Temple in Jerusalem, the epitome of the desecration of a sacred place, desecration of the sacred itself. The Lord whom we know as one who brings order out of chaos, giving meaning, direction, and purpose, seems absent in a situation where human beings are wantonly tortured and murdered, where children are gassed to death for being born to certain parents.

"Where is God now?" say the prisoners in Elie Weisel's essential book on his experience in the camps, *Night*. They have watched a twelve-year-old boy hanged for stealing bread, a hanging which, because of his emaciated condition, takes a long time. "Where is God now?" we ask with those prisoners, privileged, in a way, to share in the smallest way their despair, to feel for a fraction of a moment a situation which lasted for months and years. After the attack on the World Trade Center, we asked, "Where is God now?" a question which serves to express our grief, horror, and shock at such irrational, chaotic, and meaningless violence. "Where is God now?" is our first question; it need not be our last. When we ask that question we indicate that we are taking seriously horrendous violations of human dignity and life. We have discovered a truth about God, that our relationship to God is bound up with human beings. We cannot think of God completely in a completely separate, discreet, absolute way.

Inhumanity is properly responded to with a gesture, not with words; words fall away in the presence of a cold decision to murder. It is precisely unspeakable; what can you possibly say about it? We realize that "Where is God now?" is a question better not answered, or at least not addressed to God.

Any religious language, especially that which seeks to explain what can't be explained, is inadequate to the task of explanation, which is why religions characteristically communicate by story, narrative. Worse still is a thin and false kind of religious reassurance, that which seeks to find some good, some "silver lining," some "deeper religious meaning" in a situation like this. A rush to console, make it better, trivializes the suffering of those who died, trivializes the suffering of all innocent people. Christians might well think that quick, reassuring answers trivialize the suffering of Jesus who surely died in much the same situation as the prisoners in the camps: alone, despised, rejected. Our constant prayer might be, "Save us from the over-swift reassurance which leads to triviality of spirit."

There are no words, I think, which can adequately challenge the deadly power of evil present in such a place as those death camps, in such a movement as Nazism, or, for that matter, in the attack on the World Trade Center. If Jesus, my friend said, reflecting on the absurdity of something called "Christian" anti-Semitism, were at Auschwitz, being a Jewish man, he would have died as did every other Jew, an emaciated person in rags with a number tattooed on his arm. Jesus would have been caught with the other poor souls in the towers in New York. Would not Jesus, who shared the human condition absolutely, have asked with his compatriots, "Where is God now?" "O God, my God, why have you forsaken me?"

It occurred to me that many of our explanations and reflections on Jesus' suffering and death, some of which are quick to reassure believers that, underneath it all, Jesus was okay, at peace, are just so many words in the face of Jesus' innocent suffering and the suffering of all the innocents, especially Jesus' Jewish brothers and sisters. The best response to that suffering, as with the Holocaust, is the refusal to explain or attempt to make sense of what is devoid of sense, a refusal to make something "good" out of it. One covers his head, turns away, and weeps silently.

After talking to my friend that day at coffee, I got into my car and drove home, deeply disturbed and thinking about what we had been saying. We must be willing, I thought, to give up glib assurances, to allow Jesus to step back out of history, to be with his people, anonymous and unknown, a stranger in a strange land, to let Jesus be himself. It came to me that Christians had in some ways hijacked Jesus, taken him from where he belongs, fitted him out to live in a Gentile world.

As I drove along that day I suddenly felt closer than ever before to Jesus, even strangely warmed, as Charles Wesley said, by that presence. When I recognized the presence of Jesus with his anonymous, suffering people, pushed out of sight into the midst of humanity, I knew his presence more than ever. (I write so intimately about Jesus and my experience in a book which hopes to reach out to people of many religious orientations only because I, too, am part of a particular people, and that cannot be denied, despite all the offenses connected with it. I hope my relationship described here can be seen as comparable to my relationships with my Jewish friends, for whom I have the greatest love and respect as Jews whose faith is complete in itself. I cannot separate Jesus from his Judaism, this Jew who is present in my life.)

In his remarkable novel *Lying Awake*, Mark Salzman writes about a Carmelite nun, Sister John of the Cross, who suddenly finds herself having spiritual experiences of great power and writing wonderful, profound poetry out of those experiences. Sister is overwhelmed by these visitations of the graciousness of God, her life before having been fairly arid, dry—a common, if not often acknowledged, experience of those who live the religious life. That the aridity of her life is broken by experiences of power and wonder leaves her profoundly grateful for the gift she's been given. It seems somehow right to her that the more she is visited by God the more she suffers from terrible headaches. She figures that this suffering is part of the price one pays for a close experience of God but, being a practical sort of person, she also consults her physician about her headaches.

She discovers that the source of her terrible headaches and the source of the powerful religious experiences is the same, a small tumor in the temporal lobe just above her ear. Medical people tell her that tumors in this location have been known to produce just such spiritual ecstasies, pointing out cases in history. Her doctors offer to remove the tumor, an offer she accepts, but not without qualms. She wonders, what will she be losing?

The result is that she returns to ordinary life, the life before she received such remarkable visitations. In her restored aridity there are, however, powerful memories of graceful moments in the presence of God. Was that which seemed so real actually illusory? Or does it only seem to be illusory? Was it just that these visitations were for a purpose, and for the time-being? Was their purpose to reveal that Sister's now quite ordinary life is not so ordinary, perhaps was never so ordinary, because of what happened? Perhaps what makes life ordinary are occasional, ordinary experiences of the transcendent One.

Our ordinary lives are maybe not so ordinary because of the various experiences we've had, experiences with God and with life, experiences with the death of gods. We have had lots of experiences, insights, precious moments of knowing God, of not knowing, and of being known by God. Have they changed us? How can we be sure? Perhaps they were just fortuitous mixtures of brain chemicals. We recognize these questions and doubts as old friends and old enemies. Sometimes, like old friends, they have served us well, and sometimes, like old enemies, they are familiar, maybe even recognizable and valuable irritants.

In Salzman's novel, the new life which Sister takes up, a life which is without the certainty of God's presence, is also without, as the critic Lawrence Weschler in the *New Yorker* magazine (October 2, 2000) points out, "the vanity and futility of seeking perfection." Sister John realizes that wisdom one day when she works to clean out a fountain dedicated to the Blessed Virgin and, finished, rings a small bell which she carries in her habit. Salzman writes, "The sound cheered her, then vanished into the deep blue air, which seemed to go on forever." Weschler notes that before her operation she was certain of the sound and the deep blue air which went on forever, but now it only "seemed." She begins to accept herself as a creature, like all of us, of "seeming." God "seems" real to us at one moment, and then "seems" distant. Older people have lived through many moments of this kind, fallen away, then come back. We know the vanity and futility of seeking perfection.

God is present with us always, but always anonymous, known *and* unknown, certain and seeming. Grace sometimes overflows. Again, we are not sure of that, perhaps it only seems to overflow. One thing is sure: the easy God we knew in our youth, and in other moments throughout our life, is "seeming." It does not occur to us that knowing God as "seeming" is an important insight, one which makes us valuable in the lives of those around us.

We who have grown up with and in God can be satisfied with that "seeming" because our God seems almost always to destroy as well as to build up, as a gardener digs up the garden to prepare it for the new season. One destroys an old perfection when he sees it as a vanity and a futility. Sister John of the Cross discovered the destroying as well as the building; the destroying and building together are God. But we are always building anew with God, not trapped in the certainty of our human conceptions; we are building in the midst of seeming. Such complexity, such nuanced understanding of God is ours as we grow into the God of the living. We see the lives of our families, and our lives, as contingent, mutable, passing, and love life all the more for it. When younger people come to talk to us it is perhaps because they sense in us a depth which we will pass off as being the gift of age. But we know that God has given us richness, a richness of abandonment as well as a richness of presence.

So we say again that it is our experience as people of a certain age who are searching for our truth that God is strangely present to us in absence. We who are older and who have lived with God for many years have fallen in and out of love with God many times. And yet for me and for so many others, God is never so present as in God's presumed absence.

When one admits that God cannot be present, maybe even ought not to be present, God is often there, as she was to me in the car—not as commanding, ruling, ordering, or even making sense, but God as God, a victim with victims, God with God's people, being-itself there in silent witness with us at unspeakable, irrational horror, evil done to God's beloved people. We know God not in majesty or power, but God in God, standing before that abyss of meaning, allowing it its full depth of evil and sin. When William Sloan Coffin spoke of the death of his son, killed in an accident, he could only say, rejecting the quick reassurances and comforts of friends, "God was the first to weep that night." We are privileged sometimes only to weep with God.

I have walked through this difficult territory with you at least partially because as aging people we owe ourselves some depth, and depth comes from difficulty, from struggling with hard things. We ought not to protect ourselves from spiritual struggle. What sort of people would we be if that were our take on life? We would be bothered if all our grandchildren ate were lollipops. We would roll our eyes (mouths tightly shut) if our grandchildren were coddled. Wallace Shawn, actor and playwright, wrote of his youth, "My friends and I were delicate, breakable children and we always knew it. We knew it because of the way we were wrapped, because of the soft underwear laid out on our beds, soft socks to protect our feet." Shawn also writes, "The temptation is to be easy on ourselves, and we've all discovered that it's easier to be easy on ourselves if we're easy on each other too." Not being easy on people doesn't mean being abusive, or judgmental; it does mean holding in our minds a hope for others that is more than the hope they have for themselves.

It's important not to be easy on ourselves. The temptation for us comes from our sense of having lived through so much that perhaps it's time to be easy on ourselves. Are we saying it's time for us to stop being human? We have learned profoundly to be tolerant, accepting, but it's also a time for us to be clear about the sacredness of persons, the hope we have for them, the hope we have for ourselves.

We will not stop growing, not stop questioning, not stop wrestling with the God whom we know in absence as in presence. We will do these things not because we're cranky, ornery folks (well, not every day anyway) but because we're fully human, as human as we ever were. To be human is to be disturbed, wondering, struggling. To be befuddled by God, angry with God, to feel the emptiness of God's absence, is strangely enough one of the gifts we have to give to our ourselves, along with the hope—that, and the notion that God seems to be able to handle everything we throw at her.

4

WALKING

BACKWARD

TO WISDOM

One of the most difficult things about retiring is coming to terms with "being nobody." I've known people completely to fall apart at this moment, not knowing either what to do or who to be. Their power and responsibility are gone, and they had not realized how much that had become their identity.

We carry, whether we know it or not, the gravitas which accrues when we have embodied an institution or business. When the burden is lifted, the gravitas goes with it. The assumed wisdom which is often projected on us as senior members of a business or institution also often seems to fly away. Suddenly people neither know nor care. When I stop in to see friends at the school where I taught, I discover that the students I knew have moved on, some faculty have left or retired; I'm no longer "the parson."

Often when people retire they move their residence (I moved to my summer house) and are now citizens of a town where people have been going along quite nicely, thank you, without them. When we walk into stores or town offices, people give us the vaguely friendly look they give all strangers, not the pleasant welcome we're accustomed to in our old haunts. We feel adrift. We have gracefully, for the most part, exited our previous position; if we were lucky, we might have had some kudos heaped on us. While it might have crossed our minds to wonder where all that appreciation and thanks were ten years before, while we are being praised we are happy; but now, after the shouting dies, there is nothing except a new life to build, new paths to develop, new friends to make, new customs to be learned. We are the new girl or boy in town, and that hasn't happened to us for a long time.

I'm sure this is true everywhere in the country, but in New England, where I live, longevity counts. When he came to work at my house, an electrician, a member of one of the old Portuguese families who populated this area when it was centered around fishing, pointed out that the contractor (to whom he is related), who had moved here when he was seventeen years old, was "a tourist." Such people point out mournfully the virtues of the eighteenth-century house which occupied my lot before it almost fell apart and was moved, thriftily enough, to a neighboring town. We newcomers smile cheerfully, knowing that fifteen years from now we'll probably still be new-comers. That's different from being recognized and greeted at the drugstore, the florist, the dentist's office, and the liquor store in the town where I used to live.

Many of us have given up responsibility and authority and no longer find people listening carefully to what we say, paying particular attention, and no longer find occasions when we are asked to give our opinion. I can tell you that if I rose to speak in Town Meeting, the reception would be polite but not, shall I say, atten-tive. Doesn't anybody care what I think? The short answer is: no. And this is the correct answer. I don't know the background of the various controversies enough to make a whole lot of sense about them. A good deal of what I know about—being the chaplain and teacher in a boarding school, for example—is sim-ply not relevant to a Cape Cod town, its children, or its politics. I am not a big deal if I ever was one.

What I have, however, is what I have gained from that other time, other place, other situation, which is trans-ferable. It is the result of reflecting with a "detached concern with life itself in the face of death itself" (George Vaillant, *Aging Well*). That is, in spite of everything, what I have to offer myself and offer you, and even offer this town when I have faded in long enough. It's called wisdom. If we choose to see our-selves in this way, give up our notion of ourselves as powerful, all-knowing, and in charge, we will discover a well-spring of wisdom which can be our gift to the people around us, a gift about which we will be mod-est and unassuming.

Let us consider for the moment what a detached concern with life itself—wisdom—means in a familiar area: medicine. The mapping of the human genome means that medicine will take on a completely new look in years to come; diseases will be understood at a cellular and molecular level. However, in the light of modern advances in medicine, we should remember the doctors who served in the past who, while they worked in relative ignorance (medically speaking), possessed something which most students of medicine have come to agree is essential for healthy medical practice. That possession was their profound knowledge, perhaps *because* of their relative scientific ignorance, of the limitations of human knowledge—a kind of wisdom. Their wisdom was that they knew what they did not know.

They accepted their finitude and shared their patients' finitude, which meant that they shared their humanity. The lack of the temptation to play God—so tantalizing in medicine—paradoxically glorified their humanity. They knew the limits of their power, not only because medicine had not advanced very far (remember that it wasn't until the 1920s when a patient was statistically better off seeing a doctor than not seeing one) but also because the interior resources of the person with whom they worked were called on to understand and accept their humanity. Those old doctors, whom I am not in any way idealizing, realized that they could not know or control everything about their patients. The thoughtful ones might have had some intuitions about the reason for this, one of them being that persons are ultimately unknowable, that we are all a wonderful, precious mystery.

The characteristics of a good doctor—empathy, acceptance of those around us, integrity of the self and of the work—are the same now as years ago. Those characteristics, easier to describe than to embody, relate to "wisdom in the secret places," knowledge of the self in relation to the world. In the field of medicine this means knowledge of the limitations of medicine as well as of its opportunities. "First, do no harm," has been the doctor's creed forever, a creed which, in its acceptance of the possibility of medicine to harm as well as heal, is elegantly human. That is, it accepts human finitude; the doctor who embodies this creed does not believe that he is God. That sounds simple-minded, but as one is struck over and over again in the stories people tell of their unfortunate encounters with the medical community, it is not obvious at all. Accepting one's humanity is for all of us something of a struggle, and medical people are presented with a greater temptation than most.

I pause here to pay tribute to my own old doctor: our relationship spanned forty years until he died recently. He was an elegant man, one who chose skillfully and carefully—the root meaning of the word "elegant." In appearance, manner, and interests, which included rare book collecting and research into prescientific medicine, he was fully human in the most elegant sense. My doctor practiced medicine as an art; one also had the sense that his decisions were not so much, as it were, "driven," by tests, etc., as they were chosen (carefully) among many options. I have no prejudice in favor of older doctors; this is in no way a "young doctors are human computers" screed, because many of my young medical student and doctor friends give me exactly the same sense. I believe they are very consciously aware of their calling to elegance in the midst of their limitations. Surrounded by all the tools of modern medical science, they are intensely aware of the need to choose carefully. "Elegance," in the sense of finding ingenious and practical solutions to difficult problems, is very much part of their personal vocabulary and manner.

Human wisdom and the knowledge of God are also special kinds of knowledge which require "elegance," not "knowledge" as we often use the word, referring to what can easily be written down or communicated quantitatively. It is rather knowledge carefully and skillfully chosen, that is, wisdom gained in experiencing human triumphs and tragedies in the presence of God. It is primarily a knowledge of the self before God, the integrity which comes in recognizing that it is the self alone, vulnerable and finite, which is close to the elemental Presence, or ground of the universe. This *wisdom,* "detached concern for life itself in the face of death itself," is the kind of knowledge a doctor has when he or she recognizes personal and scientific limits as well as possibilities, the kind of knowledge of God and the self we have when we see ourselves in the light of the Eternal One. Think of it simply as part of our toolbox as human beings. It is something we know, something we have learned, perhaps painfully, of which young people, for example, can have no idea, not having lived. It's no fault of theirs; it's simply that grinding through the years teaches us something, as does, if we are lucky, laying down the "active work of life." The accumulation of wisdom is not particularly to our credit, those of us who are older; it simply happens as we observe and experience life.

Wisdom, however, is a slippery thing. Just when you think you have a corner on it, an event or insight comes along to transmute it, rebuild it into a deeper understanding, or even contradict it entirely. Occasionally the computer offers us the opportunity to "rebuild the desktop." Click on that choice and there is a great scurrying about of icons, then a sudden settling which looks, from the outside, as if some choices were being made about where to toss the various files. Then there it is, if we've been lucky everything is still easily available, but the way it's displayed and therefore the way we look at it has been radically changed. Sometimes, on the computer, and sometimes also personally, the rearrangement changes the knowledge itself because we see new possibilities, new relationships, new connections. This is parallel to the rearrangement of life as we approach aging.

We've probably all had times in our lives when we thought we had gotten it together, when life seemed, for better or worse, to be sorted out. And then, out of the blue, comes a moment, a chance remark, or an event of little or great consequence—certainly retirement and aging—and everything falls apart, "the center cannot hold," only to be rebuilt. We know what Rilke meant when he wrote about Michelangelo's statue of David, that when you see it you cannot remain the same, you must change, because, presumably, seeing or experiencing something has given you an entirely different idea of the possibilities of the human.

The sudden strangeness of a changed life after a time when everything was settled is not a particularly unusual experience. We know how different life becomes when a date is finally set for retirement. The "desktop" or pattern of life is changed completely. The person planning retirement factors a new circumstance into almost every decision, or at least adds the footnote, "I am doing this for the very last time."

When a friend was diagnosed with cancer, she noted how three little words, "You have cancer," set her life caroming instantly in a different direction. That one short sentence, indeed, that one word, meant that everything from that moment on was changed, colored in a different way. She had to change her life. A light was switched on which would never go off. Something similar happens as a result of every serious crisis or change, whether pleasant or unpleasant; we are not the same. This insight was brought to us brutally on September 11, 2001.

This is true not just because there may be trauma or suffering, but adjustment and reevaluation are involved in any change in direction. We all felt the earth shake after the horrendous terrorist attack on the World Trade Center; one of the results was for many people a reevaluation of priorities. They asked themselves what was really important. One wonders if there will be a turn from the heavily ironic, "post-modern" worldview so characteristic of the late eighties and nineties of the last century. A moment of history may cause a change in the intellectual "take" on culture. Mockery, cynicism, deliberate lack of direction, and denial of meaning are suddenly out of place in a world of sudden life and death. Deliberate chaos demonstrates that a stance of absolute relativism is flimsy ground on which to build human life.

Some years ago I bumped into an old friend from high school, a superb academic theoretician of music and a remarkable jazz musician. He is a kind of polymath, a brilliant man who knows an enormous amount about a few things, and a good deal about almost everything. I thought at the time that I "knew what I liked," especially in music. In the midst of this conversation, adopting the ironic, piercing manner of our high school and college conversations, he drawled, "I see you're still getting your taste from the *New Yorker.*" Crunch.

The remark caused me to this day to question in what ways I surround myself with ideas and things which are derivative of the taste-makers, not expressions of my true self. It bothers me that I have a hard time appreciating the latest poets, post-modern novelists, film makers, and contemporary artists, so I make sure that I expose myself to their work; I don't want to get my taste from anyone, certainly not from my clever musician friend, so I am quick to interrogate myself about my enthusiasms.

Living most of my life amongst young people has enabled that process because they are always challenging what is accepted, pushing the borders of taste, a habit which is sometimes obnoxious, sometimes helpful, in revealing where what is called "taste" really comes from. Living day-to-day with college and boarding school students has also helped to keep my mind open because everyone knows that I am a person *without a competitive bone in my body* (this statement elicits shrieks of laughter from my friends), and I hate it when my young friends know or appreciate something I don't. I draw the line at heavy metal rock bands.

My old friend's chance remark has kept me in many ways from regarding myself as a finished person, in the sense of being closed or complacent. I still read the *New Yorker*, by the way, and it's stood me in good stead.

In the same way we have all, I hope, had experiences of a moment which changed our former understanding radically, when we suddenly became aware of the fact that our knowledge was partial, that we understood as a child when we were being called to understand as an adult. One can be eighty years old and still be a child in terms of wisdom. On the other hand, and by way of encouragement, it occurs to me that it's awfully hard to be twenty years old and understand as an adult. Retirement is our opportunity to interrogate our former understandings, our wisdoms, and see if they stand up when we are in a different place in life.

When I was a very young clergyman making pastoral calls through the parish, I dropped in one day on a family whom I knew through church attendance and various meetings. I liked their easiness and rather exuberant friendliness. They were the sort of family one planned to visit at the end of an afternoon for a relaxing conversation, sure that here, after all, none of the multitude of problems and issues of the rest of the day would arise. I sat in the kitchen while the wife and mother began preparations for family dinner, a mug of coffee in front of me. We chatted about their children, her interests in the neighborhood, all the typical 1950s things one talked about. I remember thinking (I was very young) that they were some sort of perfect family. Then there was a rattle at the door and the husband entered, swaying, reeling, blinking, stoned drunk. His wife put both hands on her head. "Oh, God," she said, "I just knew you'd come home like that tonight with him here." I realized how blind I'd been, how stupid, how little I knew about them, how partial my understanding had been, how partial and superficial I'd been. It was long before the days of "intervention" and "enabling," and "denial" was a word I'd read about in books and discussed in seminar. I fled.

Well, that's the way we grow up, to understand that things can change very rapidly and very seriously and that we understand only in part.

So I've come to question accepted, customary ways of thinking, because wisdom is slippery. Just as I ask if I'm really seeing what's there to see, I question if the wisdom handed over customarily is valid. I wonder if

I have neglected to listen with an inner, an understanding heart. What difference does not being in
charge mean? The questioning self, neither satisfied
nor finished, not simplistically clear about the exact
nature and description of virtue, though sure that
virtue and virtues exist, stands us in good stead. One
of its gifts is the sure sense that we are finite, not God,
not ever, and that we do not perfectly know the mind
of God, or the purpose of God in us. We will be saying that for us, too, there are meanings and directions
yet to be revealed. Our openness to the new, our questioning of the easy and the customary, will reveal our
acceptance of our finitude and our trust in the One
who stands above all human endeavor, all human
understanding, all human wisdom, all human knowledge, whose ways and thinking are not our ways.

I have had to develop a questioning spirit, to be somewhat mistrustful of what seems to be obvious, to wonder if what is recommended as true, perfectly true,
clearly and obviously and simplistically true, is in fact
an eternal verity. To my chagrin I have discovered that
I have to apply this critical spirit as much to those who
agree with me politically as those who disagree.
Political or spiritual notions may be true enough in
some ways, not in others, or perhaps not quite true
enough. It might be partial or childish knowledge, not
mature, adult wisdom. It might be a manipulative lie.

Virtue and truth alive and met together are not some
easy motto or slogan but vibrant, turning, changing,
twisting, revealing themselves in complexity and
nuance, in shades and shadow, in light bright and dim,

in colors varying. We know God who is truth and virtue in "dappled" ways, as the Jesuit poet Gerard Manley Hopkins wrote: "Glory be to God for dappled things—for skies of couple-colour as a brinded cow; For rose-moles all in stipple upon trout that swim . . ." ("Pied Beauty"). Hopkins was so full of the changing beauty which reflected the being of God that ordinary English language was not sufficient to express his thought and he rushed to invention in order to communicate, as in the coined word "couple-colour."

Great poets such as Hopkins and John Donne understood that truth has depth, is understood on different levels, and must be approached with respect and openness. Donne writes:

> . . . doubt wisely; in strange way
> To stand inquiring right, is not to stray;
> To sleep or run wrong, is. On a huge hill,
> Cragged, and steep, Truth stands, and he that will
> Reach her, about must, and about must go;
> And what the hill's suddenness resists, win so. . . .
>
> "SATYRE III"

The depth, power, and truth of virtue does not change, but what we know of it, its shape and tenor, is different in different times. What we joked about in 1952, when I graduated from high school, is different from what we joke about now, and we are, I think, embarrassed when we recall some of those old jokes. That embarrassment inclines us to question all our joking, while at the same time our sense of the absurdity of much of life pushes us to make jokes. We know so much more clearly today that words change things, words make things happen, and the remark, "It's only a joke," or, "Just kidding," can cover hatred and abuse. We ponder Sigmund Freud's insight that there are no jokes, knowing at the same time that there are jokes aplenty, and good ones about the cigar-smoking Freud himself. If we recalled topics of conversation and remarks we made in high school and college, we would blush red with embarrassment. I am thinking especially of the racially prejudiced, misogynistic, anti-Semitic, and homophobic language and stories which were rife. We think of them and then remember Selma or Birmingham or the night we heard than Dr. King had been shot. We know of the battered women who live in our communities, of survivors of the Holocaust whom we have met, the million and half Jewish children under eleven who died. We think of the jokes about gay people and remember Matthew Shepherd hanging on a fence. We think, "There is no truth in us."

It is also true that "everybody did it." This is not repeated here as an excuse, but to point out that it was certainly unquestioned, indulged in by many people of great public responsibility and dignity, the "leaders of society," and it passed as the wisdom of the day. Today we would not repeat the scandalous conversations of the earlier part of the twentieth century and certainly not call them Virtue. But at the time they were unquestioned, regarded perhaps not as Wisdom, but as true, or true enough for respectable people to repeat them over and over so that they achieved the stature of "everybody says it," the big lie which becomes the truth. When we treat as immortal the opinions of the people of the past, we can't pick and choose what fits today and ignore the fact that much of what was held then we would regard as wrong. Recently some scholars have pointed out what was known but not recognized for so long, that slavery in the United States wasn't an exclusively Southern phenomenon. It was part of the warp and woof of New England culture, so there is no foundation for a stance that one area of the country was more virtuous regarding slavery than any other.

When we identify Virtue with the accepted values of the past, we are making those who possessed them into God. They were not God, and neither are we. When I look over the heap of discarded ideologies and beliefs that characterized my life, I affirm that there are no Gods but One. I also remind myself to watch out for people who deify themselves and their thinking for their own political ends, including, by the way, myself.

What "wise men" think has changed. We are not fully mature unless we have thought better about many things. So some of what was once "the common wisdom" or "common sense" we know today to be shameful, a good deal of it rubbish. The publication of a book or article which purports to be a compendium of Virtue reveals an author with a superficial view of what it means to be human, grounded in a ideology which is God-denying, no matter what it purports to be.

It seems to me preposterous to suggest that virtue is a done deal, not if we are serious people who have been engaged in the changed and changing life of the twentieth century, not if we recognize that human beings are finite, limited, and not if we recognize that we are not the God who is Wisdom Herself. We are flawed people, people who make mistakes, people who have lived hard in history and been scarred and changed by it. Not to change with our changing history means that we think that we are somehow immortal (take a look in the mirror) or that we are perfectly in touch with God (live a little). Life, with all its failed gods of race and clan, has taught us that of all the things we are, immortal is not one of them. We are not perfectly in touch with the truth, even if Truth is perfectly in touch with us.

Human finitude is our glory and our tragedy. It is our wisdom. We are not God, but ourselves, divinely, as it were, human. If we look back over our lives and count the mistakes, the errors, the stupid decisions, the idiotic remarks, the carelessness with our lives and with others in which we have all taken part, we know ourselves as human. When we admit to ourselves our cupidity, self-centeredness, and blindness we become, paradoxically, credible. The fact that we make the same mistakes over and over again becomes not just pathetic, but in its milder forms typical and almost reassuring. When friends came to visit me a while ago, the long-suffering wife cautioned her husband to make sure he picked up everything and packed it in his suitcase. "You left your coat the last time we stayed at someone's house," she said. "Look around now and pick up everything." A day later I was at the post office mailing him the handkerchief he left on the bedside table. That silly incident sums up our humanity in all its nuttiness and in all its glory.

Some of the virtues recommended in an earlier age might possibly have served, or served some people, well. But we have enough experience to know that a superficial understanding will not do. We must learn to interrogate the conventional and the accepted more than ever, and make a stride for truth, however nuanced and careful. We can be witnesses to Truth as long as we understand that we are not Truth. Our aging gives us the impetus and the chutzpah to do this.

Facing retirement and aging means that we can know God's limitlessness in our finitude. Insofar as we accept the limits of our knowledge, our "childishness," we know the possibility of perfect Wisdom. We realize that "childishness" and "maturity" are on a sliding scale, and while we might have more maturity than our grandchildren, we are hardly people of a perfect maturity. As long as maturity just means "older," we're fine; but if it means "wiser," we do best to step back and smile modestly, knowing that silence is probably our best chance to appear to be wise.

From Cain to Hitler and Pol Pot, humanity's curse has been arrogating to itself the role of God, judge over life and death. One of the gifts we hold in our hands is our humanity, our finitude, our not-knowing, our being absolutely sure of absolutely one thing: we are not God, not now, not ever. Our aging and retirement confront us with the certainty that we never were and aren't God. This wisdom strips away our accumulations and allows us knowledge of our own personal wisdom. Aging involves decline, but now we see that aging also involves growth and a true appreciation of who we are and what we have—knowledge of the self, wisdom, our limitations in the face of death and in spite of decline. We bring that spirit into the activities of our age, and many of us find that we are at least as effective, and certainly as happy, in the work we do in every way because we are people of a certain age.

5

Aging People

Make a

Difference

s we reach this certain moment in our lives when the intensity of the bustle of work life either lessens or ceases, or at least changes direction, we have the mental space and time to consider and reconsider some of the spiritual baggage we've been carrying, like the decongestant we tossed into our toilet kit years ago and have never cleared out despite its being expired years ago. Maybe it's time to repack for this new kind of trip we're on.

A moment or incident can reveal the true character of ways of thinking which we accepted all our lives, leading us to question what seemed so real, so solid, so given. We have all experienced moments when the accepted and conventional are revealed to be neither as full of common sense nor as benign as we had always thought. We think back over our lives and wonder, "What have I done? What could I have been thinking?"

God comes to us at the strangest moments and asks us to turn, to repent, to change our thinking. We learn to look for God, and the insights God brings, at the strangest times, when our guard is down, when we are open to creative new thoughts. These are the occasions of the God of the future, of the living, God casting down and building up, destroying in order to make all things new.

Here are two moments in my life which made me think outside the envelope, beyond the social attitudes which they challenged. These are my stories; you may recall crucial moments in your life when you realized something very important about yourself, about other people, about yourself in the presence of God, something to think about as you age.

It was a simple weekend and a simple story told me by a student about the weekend which led me to an inescapable conclusion. I was a cross-country running coach, sharing that duty with a remarkable young woman who was not only a formidable athlete, in her day reaching toward the Olympian level, but also an excellent history teacher—difficult, demanding, deeply committed to her students. While her expertise in athletics was not in running, she was an excellent coaching colleague, working with both boy and girl runners, and as demanding on the race course as in the classroom. We were a good combination—in a way, good cop and bad cop; I was all avuncular, kind, quietly supportive; she was tough, demanding, loudly supportive. We were both profoundly and deeply competitive but also, we hoped, humane and sensible. It is also true that we were both verbal people. While it has been my fate seldom to be at a loss for words, it was said of my colleague, affectionately, that she never allowed one word to serve where five hundred would do. And she carried herself, young as she was, like a coach who knew her business, because she did.

One weekend in the running season a graduate of the school asked me to perform her wedding ceremony. The race which was on our schedule for that day was not with a school in our league, so, after talking about it, my colleague and I decided that I would put on my clerical hat and perform the wedding and we would find a student to be my colleague's assistant, to take on himself or herself the conscious burden of organizing, looking out for people, making sure we brought home all our equipment. (Making sure also we brought home all our runners—more difficult than it sounds, but high on the list of things to watch out for, especially if you have left a student, as I once did, in Connecticut, two hundred miles from home.)

We chose as assistant coach for that day a student I'll call Walker, a very tall, lean senior. Funny and serious at the same time, and at the right time, Walker suffered from a chronic knee problem and, to his great frustration, had been told he was not to run for a couple of weeks. He was a smart, sensitive, alert kid, just the sort to be assistant coach to my colleague. Though tall and well-built, he still looked very much like the eighteen-year-old he was.

When I got back from the wedding, Walker found me and told me the story. The team was great, he said, everything went well, everyone appeared on time (with running shoes, a miracle), and the bus left on schedule. They arrived at the other school and spotted the host coaches waiting by the gym. Walker, who was riding in the front seat with the coach (coaches always ride in the front seat, partially because they can't stand to be part either of the merriment or the mourning in the back, nor can they stand listening to the music), grabbed the medical kit and swung out of the door, feeling very much his responsibility. My colleague, the female coach, followed. They walked toward the opposing coaches who approached them, stuck out their hands, walked past the female coach to Walker, shook his hand, and said, "Welcome, coach."

I can remember Walker telling me the story the next day and reliving the moment when the thirty-year-old, passionate, verbose Olympian had been ignored as coach in favor of an eighteen-year-old boy. No teenager wants to be anywhere near that sort of adult confrontation, and he was physically directly in the middle. Walker was also smart enough to know that what was being acted out was, in a way, stereotypical "male" behavior. In that moment he was even more aware than usual of his gender.

Walker described the scene the way people talk about a traffic accident. As in a nightmare, he could see it coming, the inevitability; time seemed to slow down, the collision happened, moment by horrible moment, as cars meet, crash, skid, tumble, come to rest. He still seemed to be in shock. I patted him on the shoulder. "What happened after you shook hands?" Walker cast up his eyes, "She set them straight." He need say no more.

In one way it was funny because it was so stereotypical. Unable to imagine that a woman might be the head coach of a team with boys on it, unable to feature a woman having authority over men of any age, the male coaches had anointed a boy instead.

When people speak of gender, gender distinctions, and gender roles, of men's inability to share with women power and authority, I always think of this example. I can tell you that it opened Walker's eyes. "Who would choose *me*, who would think *I* was a coach," he said, "when Ms. X was standing right there?" The honest answer was, "No one would. You would be chosen only if there was no choice." For those men, no one else was there. Ms. X was invisible. She had been disappeared. And that is what grips us.

Our hair stands on end. A minor episode of a moment, soon over and forgotten perhaps, but our hair still stands on end. A human being made invisible because of her gender, an old story. In the strangeness of this event, what thoughts occur to us? Perhaps this among others: what in the background of these men made a woman in power invisible? They did not associate power with women?

We might perhaps conclude that these "coach" types were so inside their male world of athletics that they could not admit Ms. X's presence, even though their school was perfectly up-to-date on gender issues. I suspect that outside of the male world of the gym they were perfectly decent guys, helpful at home, encouraging the girls on their team. The issue is not them, it is what we make of it. Walker and I were both stunned at the insult to our friend, and we had few words that could do much good. She said to me, "I get so tired of it."

The second story. A few weeks after the confrontation at the other school I was walking down the brick sidewalks of a university town near where we lived. My wife was by my side. A man came striding toward us. He was tall, handsome, commanding, dressed in khakis, a button-down shirt, crew neck sweater, and loafers, a man of substance. (Can you guess what I was wearing? The same thing as he was wearing, the same thing I'm wearing today, fifteen years later, except for a fleece vest.)

The man seemed familiar, so when he nodded and smiled, I responded in similar form, "Hello, how are you?" We passed, a chance encounter on the sidewalk. There was a coldness next to me, and my wife's voice, "And are you close friends with the President of the University?" I laughed; familiarity with his face and stature had led me to assume that I must know him, so I had greeted him as an acquaintance.

I attended recently a session of the Supreme Court in Washington. When the justices came in they all seemed so familiar I almost expected one of them to look out, spot me, nod, and smile. But, of course, I've never met a Supreme Court justice and they don't know me from Adam. Celebrity has its price; one of them is that millions of people assume they know you. I have reflexively nodded and smiled at Senator Kennedy on the streets of Boston, realizing a second later that I have never met him. The funny thing is that he nodded and smiled back. It is laughable that I might be a buddy of the senator, or of the president of the university. Our worlds are miles apart, and not just physically.

But this is, as you may have guessed, not the end of the story. My wife worked at that university in the then fairly new field of information processing. She had just the week before organized and run a special conference on the university's response to technology. It was during the time of the desktop computer revolution, so the university was facing a crucial, controversial, difficult, and expensive decision. She had been a leading organizer and participant in the discussion.

The president of the university had also been a participant in those discussions, present throughout two days of meetings in which my wife was a prominent participant. And yet she was, on that brick sidewalk that day, invisible. The bonds of gender had led the president to speak only to me, whom, as I said, he did not know from Adam, when a significant member of his staff was ignored as she walked by my side. He might have said, "Hello, Mrs. S. Thank you for those good meetings. Who's this funny-looking fellow?" But how could a woman be important enough to greet? Better say hello to a man who was perhaps a professor whose name and position had escaped the president for the moment.

Those two events—the student being mistaken for the coach and the failure of the university president to recognize a significant member of his staff—coming quite close together, jolted me. Even though our house had always been full of conversation and thought about discrimination against women, about male prerogatives and what we called male hegemony—rule or control by men—it had never been so clearly demonstrated that sexism had the power to make women invisible. It was not personal hostility to women that was at work; it was unacknowledged, unearned, male privilege. It made two women invisible, almost in front of my eyes. And that hurt.

What happens when a person is treated as though he or she were invisible? I remember a cafeteria worker once telling me how hard it was when the people she was serving did not look at her, or talked about the food as if she were not present. We have all had experiences of being treated, perhaps at a party, as if we weren't there. Almost all of us have realized that the person we're talking to is peering over our shoulder to see who else, perhaps someone more important or interesting, is around. Perhaps I'm so boring that only I have had this experience, but I don't think so. It's not a good feeling, to put it mildly. Being disappeared in this way, treated as if one didn't exist, is a grievous injury to a human being; it feels like a denial of one's existence. Because it is.

It's clear to me that it's not enough to say simply, "Well, that's the way it is, our society is sexist to its core." On the personal level, at least, men ought to do everything we can not to take advantage of what we are given by sexism and unacknowledged, unearned privilege, like simple recognition, while women are "disappeared," as in these two examples. And part of that is reconsideration of how we think about power and authority, ultimately, how we think about God, the ground of all being, of all notions of power and authority. If there is something connected to our concept of God which causes us to treat people immorally, then we must examine carefully how we think of God. It is not God who is at fault; the problem is in our construction of the notion of God. Treating others immorally is a symptom of a fault in our conception of God. When we deny people their dignity and existence, we are revealing a glitch in our relationship to the Creator of all.

These attitudes are some of the baggage we carry, both men and women, and isn't it time to come to terms with them? Those incidents started me thinking seriously about God and gender. I had read and heard the arguments from feminist theologians and, for the most part, agreed with them. Now the pervasive nature of male references, especially in the liturgy, began to grate on me. I found myself feeling strange about referring to God over and over again as "Father." There was nothing wrong with "Father" (I'm a father, I had a father, I like fathers); it was the absence of "Mother," in reference to God, that bothered me. In other words, something was being left out; there was an emptiness, a vacancy; some thing, perhaps some one, there, but invisible, was being left out. Was all that we valued and worshiped "fatherly"? To be most explicit, is God a man, male? If we consider the metaphor "Father," referring to God and meaning "like a father," then perhaps the metaphor gets connected in our minds, gets expanded so that God is a Father like my father was a father, or I am a father. This seems to me such a narrow way to look at God that it trivializes all that God is. I trust God's fatherhood is more full, more loving, more consistent, more present than my fatherhood. God's fatherhood must, after all, break through the metaphor of "father," fill it to bursting and beyond.

In addition, the connotations and implications of referring to God exclusively as a male are powerfully evident. "God" is majestic, strong, aggressive, initiating, judging. Perhaps so, but is not God in our experience also nurturing, connecting, caring, creating, bringing life into being? Is not the creation, the beautiful, wonderful earth, the elegance of all that is, in some way revelatory of the nature of God? Is God not also our Mother as well as our Father? Have we not at moments felt drawn and bound by a love which would never let us go, to the extent of allowing us to walk away in love; and then, a love following us, a love so strong that it could endure being ignored and denied and remain rich—love which is very like a mother's love as we ordinarily think of it, only more so? We recognize aspects of God as "female" as well as aspects of God which are "male." But God is beyond all our human notions, certainly beyond our conceptions of gender. God more than fills out what it is that we have in mind when we speak of God as Father and Mother.

I am not arguing for either/or here; I am simply arguing for fullness, completion.

I remember so well the look on Walker's face as he told me about the incident at the other school, so shocked that a woman he respected (and, let's face it, feared) could be so carelessly made invisible. "It makes you feel funny about being a guy." Thus sexism diminishes men. If you are recognized just because you're a guy, when your friends are ignored because they're girls, then what sort of recognition is that? Kids desperately want to believe that things are fair, that there is some justice in the world, and they connect that with the notion that they are worth something. They sense that if some can be ignored and denied and others recognized, and for no reason, then something is basically very, very wrong. When faced with a realization of this type, young people are shaken to the core because it means to them that deep down the universe is profoundly wrong, unfair, unjust. Walker had lived through a fine example of injustice in a mustard seed, as it were. Walker and I both felt an emptiness, an abyss, a gap of meaninglessness. He was right to be upset and bothered; he had made connection with the belly of the beast.

We who have known and experienced so much of love and hatred, joy and sadness, of what has made sense and what has made no sense, need to be very careful of how we speak of God, to repack our bags with fresh ideas. We need not use sophisticated philosophical language, but we can, by how we act and speak, attempt to open ourselves to the richness of the God who is so strangely and strongly engaged in the human situation, so present in absence, so female as well as male.

This leads me to ask you to think of your grandchildren, if you have them. If you have not, think of the children who live near you or who attend religious services with you. In some ways little kids understand the things of the spirit better than older people, older people who think they know and control everything, who act as if they can put their finger on what's wrong and what's right, and be satisfied with it. Kids listen at a deeper level, to the heart, and it is our hearts that we need to purify in this instance.

Consider the effect on a granddaughter of a grandfather who is not afraid to refer to God using feminine language, who thinks her femininity so important that he is willing to break the habits of many years. Is he not saying, I care for you so much I am willing to change my comfortable ways of doing things so that you know that the special way you are you, as a young woman, is a gift to you directly from God who shares also in your femininity? Won't she know in her heart, grand pop is a funny old guy, but he sure loves and respects me? He doesn't have to go as far as he does, but he does it anyway. He's willing to go out of his way, to change, for me.

Consider the effect on a grandson of a grandmother who is not afraid to use feminine language for God, who is not afraid to honor her femaleness in front of this young man, to demand from him the respect due to all women, to be "in his face" a little. Is she not saying, I respect you so much, my boy, that I am going to demand respect from you for all women? I'm going to give up some of my comfortable ways, ways I've adopted in order to get along, to confront you a little because I know you are big enough, smart enough, man enough to deal with it. Won't he say, grandmother is something else, she's not afraid to act on what she thinks. She loves me and respects me. She doesn't have to do this, she could just do what she's done for years, but she's changing for me.

Peers have enormous influence over young people, and that influence is fairly often not very helpful to their growing up into humane people. But grandmother and grandfather have every right and obligation in the world to exercise influence, especially as they become a kind of peer. Everyone knows the old joke about why grandparents and grandchildren get along so well. They have a common enemy. A grandmother provides an excellent example of strong, independent woman-hood, a womanhood which does not kowtow to the boy as male but demands of him respect for strong women. It's important for us to respect and honor our children enough to take their spiritual lives seriously, which might mean, in this case, to present an unmis-takable reference to the female aspect of God.

I recognize that human beings are complex, that simple-minded male/female distinctions do not do justice either to the richness of our humanity or to our masculinity and femininity. The same thing is true of God: human distinctions are not always useful when applied to God. And yet part of the reason, perhaps, that women are made invisible is because we have not discovered the depth of God, the power of creation lurking in that depth. If we are open to the God who is nurturing in a strong way, creating in a powerful way, communicating with bonds of loving freedom, then perhaps we will not only have a close relationship to the God who is, but through God discover the depth of beauty and wonder in the women around us.

Here's a simple and perhaps stupid-sounding way to start. When we pray, let us try addressing God as Mother, refer to God as her, emphasize in prayers God's care for all, God's love embracing all, God's creativity flowing out to all, and God's call to all people to live in peace.

Here's something else you can do. In public prayer, quietly and respectfully replace one word for God with another. Words, after all, change things, and what we want to change is our hearts so that we engage the fullness of God. You can change from the outside in as well as from the inside out, *lex orandi, lex credendi*. Fortunately, the word "Mother" has the same number of syllables as "Father"; "he" and "she" are both one-syllable words. Things fit nicely. So you will sing, "God of Our Mothers," because after all, God was God of our mothers, of Bridget of Kildare, Madame Curie, Simon Weil, Julian of Norwich, Eleanor Roosevelt, Florence Nightingale. There are endless occasions when, without disrupting anything or disturbing anybody (Goodness, you wouldn't want to upset anyone, would you?), because after all they have a right to their own spiritual language, you can begin to set your mind straight on this and maybe simultaneously horrify and delight your children, and your grandchildren, if you have them. You will make it clear that God is beyond gender, beyond language, beyond any of the structures we have built to contain her.

It's conceivable that when we listen quietly for the God who is receptive, connecting, and creating, we will find ourselves filled with that creativity—being known by that which is receiving and accepting as much as that which is assertive—and experience what we once might have termed weakness, but which all along was the power of waiting and brooding, as women wait and brood for the moment of the fulfillment of one kind of glorious creation, the birth of a child. What might once have been termed "weak" turns out to be the embodiment of the most powerful force imaginable, the power of Being-itself.

If we are fully people of God, the boys and girls, young men and women, whom we love so much, will sense it. And if we are related to a God who knows us and whom we know in return, and the life of God in our conception is rich and full, rich and full enough to include all humanity, those kids will also sense the depth of that relationship. We will have given them the second greatest gift we could give them, the first being the parents who gave them life. We will give them the gift of the fullness of the God who creates, feeds, weeps over, and shares life with her suffering children.

It is past time for us, particularly for us men, to come to terms with whatever it is that keeps us from appreciating women. Often when there is hostility to a certain group, it grows out of fear. What is so fearful about women? Well, we say, nothing. We've lived with women all our lives, how could we find them frightening? Then where do the incessant put-downs come from? What's the source of the skittish denial of the presence of women? I wonder if it isn't because of the presence in women of the awesome power to reproduce (with a little help from their friends). It is woman who brings forth the future, quietly, silently growing under her heart, ". . . how silently the wondrous gift is given." This is tough for men, so used to being in control, so accustomed to power. There is nothing a man can do, nothing he can add, nothing much he can say; he is not in the lead, not first, but seconding, waiting in the corner.

A grandfather puts his arm around his grandson and teaches him the lesson that men must learn, finally discipline themselves to accept: this silent power of creation must be respected on every level, that it is of God, whose power is here even more than in the thunder of justice. We do not need to have constant contact with our grandchildren to be an example of respect and humility; we do need to make our presence count consistently. Perhaps a regular, long, serious letter will do when there is neither constant nor close contact.

Those of us of a certain age have the great privilege of being witnesses to a profound change in culture, a momentous act of justice. A grandfather will under-stand the moral and spiritual weight he bears. A grandmother will observe him in action with grandchildren with joy and love; she will hand down to her granddaughters, as women always have, the lore of women. She will regard her grandson with new respect as he learns of the fathering mother who is God the Holy One of Blessing. We thought we had no power; we discover the power of wisdom.

6

Cooking, Gardening,

and

Grandchildren:

Sources of Pleasure

One evening last winter I was wandering about the house putting things in order after a chaotic day of rushing off on various errands, coping with a sudden snowfall, realizing the dog hadn't been walked adequately (poodle owners will know that the sure sign of this is a curly-haired dog lying across the most traveled pathway in the house glaring at her owner), when I realized I also had to figure out something to eat for dinner. Taking care of first things first ("It's about time!" muttered the dog as she pushed by me), I returned to thinking about dinner.

Men and women who live alone will recognize this problem: we don't want to bother making a "full" meal and don't really want it, but we're hungry. We don't want to fuss, but we also know it's necessary to provide our bodies, and especially our brains, with the proper nutrients to ensure that we will function at a satisfactory level.

Most of us, retired or not, have a lot on our metaphorical plate: household maintenance, that blasted lawn, children vigilance, volunteer work, community responsibilities. Those of us who live in certain places in New England with our odd form of town government know we're obligated to our neighbors to turn up at Town Meeting several times a year to listen to those neighbors ramble on and on in the worst form of government devised except for any other. If we're not retired, we work either in or outside of the house. In the meantime we have to eat, and eat in a decently healthy way. There's no reason to look at it as hard labor or an onerous duty. A lot of us have the time, and once in a while the inclination, to think cooking something good might be satisfying in more than one way.

So there I was on that winter night, the driveway cleared, the dog finally walked and righteously snoozing on a favorite couch, the computer shut down for the evening—what should I eat? I rummaged through the refrigerator. There were the usual odds and ends, leftovers from a couple of dinner parties, half-finished this and that. Half a slice of pita bread languished in the freezer from a previous essay into hummus consumption. There were remnants of various cheeses, part of an onion, some prosciutto, a slice or two of smoked salmon, some vegetables. I grabbed a selection of eligibles and thought to build a pizza on the pita. On went the oven to its highest possible temperature, the pita was spread out on a cutting board. I picked up some fresh mozzarella which just possibly had been around for too long. No, a quick sniff discerned its essential sweetness and clarity; I cut it over the pita. There were some decent tomatoes scavenged from my favorite fruit and vegetable store in a neighboring town, the one run by a friend's daughter. This terrific young woman employs every pierced, tattooed, ragged, scruffy young person she can find, and somehow imbues them with spirit, energy, cheerfulness, competence, and a dry sense of humor. (One time I was searching in that shop for something as simple as parsley. In my usual distracted way I pawed through the various herbs, asking a young worker, was it this one which was parsley? no cilantro, this one? no watercress, this one? etc. until finally I found parsley. I thanked him, apologizing for asking so many questions about a simple herb. His response, verbally patting me on the shoulder, was, "Not at all, sir, we never learn anything unless we ask, do we?" Something which I probably said thousands of times in my teaching career. His grin told me he knew just what he was saying. You can see why I go back there.)

I sliced the tomatoes onto the mozzarella, dribbled chopped onion, some elderly zucchini, prosciutto, salmon that had seen better days, onto the tomato, and then over it all crumbled goat cheese and leftover

Explorateur, a rank soft French cheese which clogs your arteries if you even look at it. Everything was melded together with some of the hottest salsa I could find. Then came a grate or so of good Parmesan, and in it went to that furiously hot oven.

Twenty minutes of impatient waiting later, I pulled this pizza out, slapped it on a plate, and settled down to the table with the book of the day and the glass of wine I allow myself at night. I waited a while for the cheese to stop bubbling, cut a small slice from the curiously attractive mess, waited again for it to stop steaming, and ate it.

I can remember thinking, "This is heavenly."

We know heaven, and God, in just such moments, moments of deep satisfaction and fulfillment, which go far beyond the immediate need to satisfy our pangs of hunger. There is something more than refreshing about such times, as we reflect on the deep true meaning of refreshment, all things fresh and new, all things made again, born again into the wonder of the world and the creation.

Not all our experience of God is "oceanic," overwhelming. Not every religious experience is vast, and certainly mystical experience is not the property of the religious professionals or the professionally mystical. If war is too important to be left to the generals, then the experience of God is too important to be left to the mystics. God belongs, is present, to all of us and uses the most ordinary things to invite us into an experience of wonder, light, and praise, even homemade pizza with leftover toppings. And at our age we have the time to appreciate it.

At another level of culinary achievement, I was eating dinner recently with a dear friend in a famous and remarkable restaurant in Berkeley, California. We were eating their simple, fresh, natural food, the exquisite skill and thought which goes into it concealed by the lack of pretension in presentation, the uncanny casualness which conceals enormous care and professionalism, like the ballet dancer's smile, in order to allow the diner completely to relax. As we were eating the entrée, the chef, who is a friend, arrived at our table with two shallow soup plates in his hands. "The first fava beans arrived today," he announced, sliding the plates onto the table, and walking back into the kitchen.

Beans are not my thing, the result of eating too many mushy concoctions of some bean or other out of which my mother expertly cooked all flavor and vitality. "You don't know what's good," my parents would say, eating the glop. Perhaps, but I doubt it. However, in this place and with this company I knew I would have to put a good face on eating beans. I spooned some into my mouth.

And Spring burst into life on my tongue. The richness of the earth, the goodness of the creation renewing itself shouted alleluia. "Good God!" I said fervently. The cook had brought out of the bean all of its potential, allowed it to be itself in the most refreshing way. Tasting it was knowing the earth in all its beauty.

One of the signs of God's presence is the spirit of refreshment or renewal, a spirit which is present all through the world, ever available for those who will allow the world, and God, to be themselves, not coated in pretense or in an imposed order which "makes better" something which is perfect in itself, which does not gild the lily. The simple pizza, by combining so many diverse flavors, the simple dish of fava beans, by presenting one theme, testified to the goodness of all that is. We reflect that diversity, in color, shape, pattern, sound, is an integral part of creation, of God's will expressed in what is. Diversity is not just a human opportunity, it is divine reality, one of the truest expressions of God's will there could be. God in all God's simplicity, God in all God's complexity, revealed in the multitudinous patterns of the world.

Those of us who are young-old are part of that diversity. If you have ever lived in a community which is composed of people who are mostly alike, you know how refreshing it is to encounter a truly diverse community. It's a kind of relief for me, living as I do on mostly white Cape Cod, to visit New York City. The first subway ride is always a great pleasure, to see the variation of color possible in human skin, to hear the sound of multitudinous accents, the sights and sounds of God's world. It is refreshing to see the possibilities, to experience the abundance of creation.

If God is known in absence, God is also known in presence, pushing constantly through the gabble and chatter of the world to refresh and renew. This is the other side of God, known and unknown, like the other side of the moon, there but not seen, not experienced, until a certain moment when the light shines. We have intimations of God in the same way, sudden moments of light in which we discern the infinite in the finite. It's important to be mindful, to train ourselves not to be distracted by pressures of work or life from that which can give us life. Those of us who live alone particularly need to give ourselves these pleasures.

One time I was shopping in a grocery store, and time was short. I had an appointment at the school where I taught, and at the same time I was planning on entertaining a group of students for dinner and needed to pick up food. I rushed from one counter to another. In my hurry I bumped into a woman who was also pushing a laden cart. Apologizing, I turned to the meat counter, grabbed something, whipped around, and crashed into the same woman again. Another apology and off to the dairy case, an absent-minded turn, and the same woman, same collision. I was embarrassed, "You must think I'm following you," I said. She smiled, "Did you ever think I was on *your* trail?" Perhaps more than one person was shopping under deadline that afternoon; perhaps more than one agenda was being lived out.

So it isn't all about me. It takes two to tango, to crash grocery carts, two to have a moment of illumination. We might stop for a moment, even while shopping, to wonder how it is that we have such ubiquitous moments of insight, refreshment, renewal. Why is this? we ask, knowing that there never can be an answer which is complete and finished until both sides decide that all is fulfilled, complete, finished.

I have two friends who are terrific gardeners. They are the gardening equivalent of my friend who is the chef, carefully and thoughtfully planning, moving through their gardens in purposeful, economical ways. In contrast I'm the other kind of gardener. I go at it only when I notice something egregiously wrong, when I have nothing else particularly to do, or when I'm writing. A few minutes ago I wandered outside to prune a wandering rose bush only to be called back to the computer by my consciousness that I had vowed this morning to be about writing, not about anything else. But for me, as for many of us whose motto is "Any Distraction Will Do," the garden is a terrific opportunity to duck out of work.

It was years before I understood the contrast between my friends' gardens and what is called "municipal gardening," as in parks with their neat blocks of annuals and ordered designs in which the order is more important than the flowers. The epitome of this is the so-called "floral clock," in which flowers are made to look like something else, or the display in which flowers spell out words.

Municipal gardens are "interesting," but neither satisfying nor refreshing. My friends' gardens, one on the coast, one in the interior of Massachusetts, are satisfying. They look almost wild; the plants are chosen to complement one another, to lead the eye to a spot of color or a particularly deep area of shade; the leaves and the flowers are allowed to be themselves, even to grow in ungainly and sprawling ways if that's their preference. One's reaction isn't to say, "Isn't that pretty?" but to sit down, smile, and relax, allowing the garden in its artful simplicity to refresh the mind and the heart.

Why do those fava beans taste of all outdoors, of spring itself, of the renewal of the earth? Why could an ordinary chef not re-create at will that moment of extraordinary flavor? The partial answer is that the great chef knows that when the beans arrive in the kitchen there is only an hour or so of potential greatness, knows out of experience and intuition how to put them to heat and when to remove them. Nothing explains the connection between my tongue, my brain, my memory, my openness to the spirit. Why does a simple pizza open to us the mystery of the universe?

The other day I came across a granddaughter sitting at a kitchen table eating dry cereal of a kind which I did not recognize. It had been dumped on the table in front of her. She ate it steadily, not hurrying, grasping each morsel in a chubby fist and chewing it thoughtfully. As I sat down to watch, she looked over, picked up a piece, paused for a moment, then wordlessly and solemnly handed it to me. I put it in my mouth and realized that it was indeed delicious, a graininess of grain. "That's delicious, Lucy. What wonderful cereal. Thank you." She turned and looked at me with her great round eyes, and smiled. She doesn't have a whole lot of words at this point and at that point didn't need any. We sat together and enjoyed the cereal, building our connection without words. Whenever we share food with someone, our hearts cannot help but overflow with love and our minds are cleansed and refreshed by this simple gesture.

If all our time with grandchildren is programmed to the second ("I'll pick him up at seven for the baseball game, we'll run by for a burger, be home by 9:30"), we'll never have a chance to share with the kids the wonder of the world. It's a good idea to celebrate wonder, not with a lot of language, what we call "God-talk," but by simply sharing our marvel at the graciousness of the world. If we hurry to our seats in the baseball park we never get a chance to indicate to the grandson or granddaughter how much we love that wonderful moment of coming out of the entrance tunnel and seeing the field so brightly lit, so magically green, the crowd gathering, the murmur of the "voice of baseball."

The same thing goes for all the other evidences of the presence of God renewing and refreshing the world, evidences which are available to us if we open our eyes, inner as well as outer.

Even moments which are not conventionally peaceful can be satisfying, an insight which can apply to struggling with a crossword puzzle or seeing a deeply moving and disturbing play or film. We know that something more is being said to us, beyond plot or even characterization, perhaps that a work of art is struggling with "why." *Hamlet* and *Death of a Salesman,* for example, reach a level beyond explanation, beyond disquisitions on Shakespeare's mind or

Arthur Miller's politics, beyond academic discussion of tragedy. These plays ponder the mystery of life, why we are placed in history, why we are dealt the hand that life gives us. They don't give us obvious, ready, or easy answers, but ponder the mystery. "Attention must be paid," says Willy Loman's wife. The same refreshing depth present in the brightly lit baseball field, the fava bean, the pizza, the hazelnut, the garden, glows under the action in these works of art.

When we struggle with the "why" of life, when we pay attention, we engage the agony of the human struggle and we are led to a profundity not present when we simply move through the maintenance gestures of life. Even though we may never reach an answer, the struggle—its insights unspeakable, unpredictable—is often satisfying, in a strange and wonderful way, refreshing, perhaps because we have seen the issues in a completely different light, from the inside, not the outside. As we empathize with the characters in the play, the gardeners, the chef at his stove, we touch the wonder and mystery of the universe.

Let me add also that struggling with puzzle and mystery is, in fact, very good for us. Exercising our brains in that way, as in working with our brains to understand new ideas, is very good for that terrific organ which can become rusty with disuse. Studies show that challenging the brain keeps it on its toes.

So it's not only a good idea, it's good for us to be about wonder and mystery, feelings and apprehensions which come long before formal language about God, pointing out moments and thoughts which are satisfying to us. We call ourselves to be mindful, of the clouds, the breeze, the beach, the city, the plants in the garden, the architecture of the buildings around us.

We don't need to carry on a scientific, art historical, or philosophical conversation. We just need to be mindful about our feelings of renewal and satisfaction before the wonder of the world and the brooding presence of God. There are times when talking is superfluous. You receive and then hand a piece of cereal to a child and act out giving, receiving, and blessing.

Mick Jagger sang long ago "I Can't Get No Satisfaction," in its own way deeply moving as the theme of those who fruitlessly look for satisfaction in the world of possessions and fame. We seldom think about what is really satisfying and renewing to us and sharing that. It can be simple things: a walk on the beach in the morning, a long bicycle ride, or a piece of cereal handed to us by a child. It can be in works of art of great complexity. They have in common authenticity; they are true to themselves, to what they are. The chef brought out the simple glory of fresh fava beans; essentially what he did was know how to get out of the way and allow the flavors of the bean to develop, to be enhanced with the treatment to which he subjected them and the materials with which he surrounded them. The object was never to disguise but to reveal.

So how important it is for us not to disguise our sense of wonder, our feeling of the close presence of God, but to reveal it, less in words than in actions, responses, reactions. The world still has a lot of pleasure in store for us.

A friend speaks of his mother as "the Queen of Disapproval." There are many among us young-olds who operate as kings and queens of disapproval. They look for all the things that could be wrong and feed on their disapproval. Nothing is right in art, music, education, politics. I was at a meeting the other night with a woman who announced, as if it were the God-given truth, "We all know that the schools are terrible." I thought of the teachers in our community who work so hard and give so much of themselves to their students. I remembered that the local high school had done very well on the state-required tests. Whether we thought those tests were a good idea or not, still and all, the school had done well. They couldn't be so terrible. But the Queen of Disapproval could find no good in them, or, to tell the truth, in much of anything. Those of us who have been teachers will not sit passively by in the name of politeness when our good colleagues are slandered. It's such a temptation at our time of life to let such things pass. Fortunately we have learned through experience how to disagree in a cheerful, but pointed, way.

In his extraordinary novel *Ironweed*, William Kennedy writes a fantasy scene set in a cemetery where the dead are alive in their deadness. The lead character's mother eats the roots of the dandelions which grow down into her grave, ". . . [she] wove crosses from the dead dandelions and other deep-rooted weeds; careful to preserve their fullest length, she wove them while they were still in the green stage of death, then ate them with an insatiable revulsion." In her death as in her life, she is in love with disapproval, bitterness, and revulsion.

There is a vast temptation to stand in judgment, to regard changes in the world with "insatiable revulsion," to see no good in anything new, to be suspicious of everything, to deplore whatever there can possibly be to deplore. But we are called, I think, to communicate to those around us the freshness and richness of the world, "the dearest freshness deep down things." We can't communicate that unless we have opened ourselves to God in such a way that we have known that freshness ourselves.

In being mindful of the wondrous possibilities of the world and the gracious presence of God, we come upon a resource of renewal and refreshment in ourselves which can cleanse us of some of the bitterness of our past, and open us to vast, refreshing possibilities for ourselves. What we want is the dearest freshness of God, the cleansing and renewing power of God, the possibility of the fava bean, the glory of the pizza.

Let those of us who have experienced so much of life be a resource ourselves of pleasure and refreshment for the people with whom we live. Let us enjoy our grandchildren in such a way that they receive challenge and delight from us. Let us challenge our neighbors to be more hopeful than they could imagine about themselves. Let us not deny ourselves the richness and pleasure of God's presence and creation.

7

THE DECLINE

OF THE

BODY

I f the body is the temple of the Holy Spirit, as scripture says, then what happens when the roof, or worse, the cellar, springs a leak? One of our tasks as the not-quite-aged is to deal with this now somewhat creaky instrument of action.

I grew up a non-athletic child, despite, or perhaps because my father was a natural athlete who could pick up any sport in a very short time. I remember struggling as an adult with tennis. There always seemed to be one more important aspect of the game than I could remember. If I remembered not to swing from my elbow, I forgot to move my feet; if I moved my feet, I forgot to bend my knees. But I had progressed a little and trusted myself at least to play with people at my level or just a little above when one day my father came out East to visit. The house we were renting had access to a tennis court, so I went over with my daughters to hit the ball around while Dad watched. "Let's see if I could do that," he said, and walked onto the court to hit a perfect forehand. This was the story of my life, with which a psychoanalyst could have great fun. But why bother?

So, probably for good reason, I stayed away from sports—little Oedipus is smart enough to avoid a sure loser. Then, sometime around the mid-sixties, running became popular and I was one of the first to join the throng. Running required no hand-eye coordination, which recommended it to people like me, and also promoted then an ideology of non-competitiveness which also recommended it to people like me who were horribly competitive but completely incompetent. I ran for more than twenty-five years until a famous podiatrist said, "If you don't stretch for half an hour before and after you run, you'll have to have hip replacements." It occurred to me that perhaps running had been a bad idea after all. Still, I did enjoy it. I remember with fondness running through the gorgeous countryside around the school where I taught and my time as an incompetent but horribly competitive cross-country running coach and the wonderful student athletes with whom I got to work.

Surrounded by athletic people at school, I walked a good deal and rode a bicycle through the trails of Cape Cod in the summer but felt that my athletic days, such as they were, were over. However, some years after the podiatrist's proclamation, I was sitting at home reading and restless on a Sunday afternoon, knowing somehow that this inertness was not me and I ought to be exercising, when I realized that my school had just built a fabulously expensive gymnasium (when gyms are fabulously expensive, they're called Athletic Centers) with a cushioned running track which was, for all I knew, going to waste. Being a miserly sort of person who can't stand anything going to waste, I threw on some shorts and dug out running shoes thinking that, if I were careful, and if I stretched, I could work off some stress and fill time that I wouldn't use productively anyway.

This worked for a while and my students even appreciated the slow, careful progress I made. "Way to go, Mr. Smith," they'd say as they streaked by. They thought I was being an example of maturity and care, while I was of course running full steam in order not to appear completely feeble. One of my daughters gave me a heartbeat monitor so I could do all this scientifically. There is nothing like a toy to help a man get about his business.

One day, however, one of the crew coaches, a tri-athlete and a good friend, stopped me. "You know," he said, looming in all his youthful muscular healthfulness, "if you just do cardio work, that's fine, but as you grow older you need to think about other things. If you built some muscle you would find that lean muscle mass burns more calories than fat and it would be easier to lose weight, and if you work muscle against bone it will keep your bones strong." He proposed, entirely out of the blue, a simple weight-lifting regime which would accomplish some of those goals. What a wonderful thing to have young friends who care about you this much! How terrific to be able to learn something from people younger. It has been noted (in George Vaillant's *Aging Well*, an excellent book on aging) that it is a healthy and ordinary thing to move from mentoring young people in our work-life to making them our friends and learning from them. As our friends begin to fall, we make a new social circle from the younger generation, or from our grandchildren. Relieved of the pressures of work, we enjoy them and also learn from their insights and their embrace of the changing world. They also come in handy for hooking up the VCR and the computer.

So I began to follow my younger friend's recommendation, lifting modest weights every other day, and working on the elliptical trainer (a weird device which uses a running stride but avoids the pounding of either running on a track or a treadmill—my hip joints and knees thanked me). I found myself getting somewhat stronger.

As time went on, my retirement loomed and I moved to Cape Cod and thought to look around for a gym where, I reasoned, I could continue with this routine and give myself not only a healthier and more vital young-old age, but also work off some of the stress and anxiety I seem to have a genetic need to collect. I found a gym (definitely not an Athletic Center) in Provincetown, a ways from where I live, but an easy drive.

And here, after a while, I found a trainer who, after a long consultation and questioning, devised a somewhat more challenging and diverse routine, based on a three-day schedule. After a while the other denizens of this gym have come to recognize me, not hard to do since I'm twenty or thirty years older than most of them, and don't have the remarkable musculature many of them sport. Since it is Provincetown, many of the people who are fellow gym rats are gay and lesbian. In Provincetown this orientation is assumed, as is an open attitude, so conversations are frank. I have found that I am learning from people younger than I, and none more poignant than when the manager of the gym, a thoughtful man who acts as unofficial rabbi for the area, in the course of a conversation in which I offered to help his ministry in any way I could, pointed out to me, "Jack, you have to remember that many of these people have suffered a lot from religion." There is a lot to think about in that remark.

And so I have gone on my way, laughing when I reach for a fifteen-pound weight just as the enormous man next to me reaches for an eighty-five-pound weight, admiring the stretching routine of a dancer, sharing a smile with someone my age. But through it all, I am slowly and carefully building lean muscle mass, strengthening my bones, building reserves of energy. This all keeps me going, helps with the occasional down moments, which I have like any person who lived a very public life, but who now lives a very private life—that is, who is no longer God. Any workout is worth, I think, every minute of time and energy I put into it. I know that I'm not an athlete, never was, and never will be, but I go to the gym and do my routine.

My activity is in dialogue with what is inevitably the decline of my body. Along with many other people of a certain age, I have refused to take that decline, as it were, lying down. If I'm going to decline, I'll face it with the regular and consistent exercise of my body in the company of the gay men and women who surround me in the gym in Provincetown.

"All your works praise you, O Lord," says the psalmist (145:10). It seems odd for us to apply that verse to our aging, declining bodies, drooping and occasionally dripping; but our bodies are still marvelous. Not to put too fine a point on it, even the decline of the body is marvelous and fascinating. The process of aging is linked to the inability of cells to reproduce themselves indefinitely. As the years go on, the process becomes more and more chancy, more and more cumbersome, less and less inevitable. So there is some scientific basis to the biblical fourscore years; there seems to be a kind of limit built into our metabolism, and we all come to it, the tri-athlete, the gym body-builder, the marathoner, the duffer, we all come to it. But the young have not yet come to it, and we love them for that and for their remarkable resilience.

The extraordinary process of cell division is why a young person can be injured and recover so much more quickly than people of a certain age. One of my students, just graduated from college, was in a terrible, tragic accident while traveling in Patagonia. Another graduate, a lovely and promising young man, did not survive that terrible car wreck, but this fellow did, even though several vertebrae in his neck were broken. (He learned a month or two after the accident that he had broken the C4 vertebrae, about which there is a medical mnemonic, "C4, breathe no more." It was a fairly breathless moment when a nurse tossed that one at him.) In addition to that, and at least as serious, was the fact that his skull was fairly crushed in the accident. He told me about the neurosurgeon picking splinters of bone from his brain. Thinking of that can, he agreed, tend to concentrate the mind.

The accident was in early November. When I saw him in mid-January, he was walking, albeit with a cane, speaking and thinking almost completely clearly. He still had a ways to go, but youth, athleticism, and an indomitable spirit will carry you a long way. Those of us who are older simply don't have the cellular power to recover in that way, which is why that ankle is still sore, if you're wondering.

But we can do things to help. While some of us are genetically gifted and still run, play tennis, etc. at an advanced age, others will engage in less demanding activities. It's the activity that's important, not whether we run faster, lift more, or plant more extensively. We do all we can and allow the natural limits to slow us down as time moves on. All God's works are marvelous. That we can do these things as well as we can is just another evidence of the loving care with which the world was made; that we can no longer do them as well as younger people is evidence that there are limits to everything.

So if all God's works are wonderful, and our bodies are wonderful, what's our problem with facing that truth about ourselves? Most of us refuse to accept a sentence to a rocking chair, so there are lots of things to do, but the further truth is the truth of limits, a truth developing power as we push our way through the years. Those of us "of a certain age," the young-old, are not immediately faced with this truth of limits, but we need to acknowledge it, even as we read the obituaries. (Do you remember laughing at your parents for reading the obituaries?)

The one word upon which I have not put much emphasis here is "decline," but God, and we, must love also the truth that our bodies decline, are limited, and indeed end. And there is wonder in that decline and in that end as they are in dialogue with the assertion, "All your works praise you, O Lord." As we exercise we express an attitude toward the world: to enjoy it and preserve it while we are able to care for it, and then willingly and lovingly give it up, to face the end not, I suppose, without regret, but with the certainty that there is a kind of truth here too, that this work of God praises her too.

If we are lucky we will have, as George Vaillant says, invested our selves in forms of life and work that will outlive the self—in gardens, in commercial endeavors, in relationships with the young, in civic projects where we live, in creating moments of beauty and fun for other people, in acts of service which have made the lives of others easier. We need not worry about what happens after the limit is up, because that is in the hands of God. God is notoriously not one about whom worrying seems to be relevant. The decline of the body is a sign, some would say, a heads-up; we plunge into this adventure as we have plunged into the rest of our life because this decline, and fall, are also part of life, as death is paradoxically a part of life, not looming immediately, but nudging us to be ready, come what may.

In *King Lear* the abused son Edgar addresses his abused father thusly, "Men must endure their going hence, even as their coming hither: Ripeness is all. . . ." We could easily see ourselves as people who are ripe, *à point* as the French would say about a cheese, just right. And then there is a point beyond. God loves the truth that we all go hence. Struggle as we might, ripe as we are, we know that eventually we will come to love that truth too.

8

LIVING LONG

IN THE

LAND

Sitting at my desk the other day, staring at the computer, not doing much, as usual, I happened to look out of the window and notice, down in the wintry garden, a particularly scraggy bunch of dead flower stalks that had not been cleared last fall. I am at best an eccentric gardener, not at all like some of my friends who nurture carefully planned plots and borders, coordinating colors and textures, trimming and pruning, weeding, arranging, and rearranging. As a gardener I am everything I deplore about contemporary culture: impatient, distracted, nonrenewable, seeking quick and easy results, impressed by the latest discoveries. Worst of all, and I confess this with a heavy heart, *I do not follow through.* Thus the flower bed allowed to wither and die and not

carefully cleared away to wait the planting and nurturing of spring.

So I threw on a coat, gathered the dog and some clip-
pers, and went out into the February chill (I should
say here that many writers will do *anything* to avoid
work, so this is not particularly unusual behavior) to
do the right thing finally. As I snipped and snapped
away I suddenly began to notice something startling,
given that it was the first week in the second month of
the year. There was a flash of green at the base of the
plant I was working on. Looking more carefully and
clearing away dead leaves, I realized that next summer's growth had already started down there, some
shoots had sprung up, albeit in a tentative way.

Drawn now to looking, I walked around the yard
checking various growing things, and realized (surely
this is old hat to gardeners who pay attention) that
nearly everything was beginning, starting up. The
buds were securely set on the crab apple tree, the roses
had popped shoots, the lilacs were well on their way,
and even the daffodils and tulips had stuck a tentative
feeler above ground. I live on Cape Cod, which often
has mild winters compared to the rest of
Massachusetts, but still and all, I thought, while we
were sleeping or huddled inside near the fire, curled
up with a good book, deciding that the dog didn't
need as long a walk as usual because of the snow and
cold, while we were avoiding and denying, the flowers
and plants had started their engines and gone to work.
Not only that, they were unafraid of the cold to come,
hardly bothering about the few inches of the snow that

would fall the next day. These little guys are tough, alert, and aware.

Reminds me of my grandchildren. While I am doting over the babe in arms, wondering if she looks like Aunt Martha or Cousin Sadie, the kid is taking a measure of the people and things around her. A six-month-old grandchild thoughtfully measures the distance between couches in the living room and pulls herself up in preparation for making the jaunt from one to the other just two months later. Who knew? Another at four is impatiently and bitterly aware he can't read words, more than ready to get about the business of reading. I'm sure that his thinking is that if he could do the job of reading himself he would not need to hassle one of us to read to him, much as we enjoy it. Then he could have the independence (glorious independence) of reading whatever book he wants when he wants to. Whether it is getting about, walking or crawling, or talking or reading, grandchildren are taking the measure of the task long before we think they are ready.

We tend to underestimate the toughness of plants and kids, their resilience, the power of their push to the future. I'm not arguing for cruelty to children, but simply underlining what parents learn: children seem to be able to deal with many obstacles and glitches far more wisely and routinely than we thought. Their eyes are on the future, leapfrogging easily over what we think of as barriers. One wonders occasionally if the concentration on children and their needs in our society doesn't have more to do with parental problems than children's needs. I am perfectly aware that children can be deeply and even permanently hurt by childhood injuries and traumas, but I'm talking about most kids most of the time. We've all seen the child who broke a leg or an arm adjust almost immediately to the cast and figure out a way to play around the obstacle. The immediate problem is just something to deal with in order to get on with the important business of living into the future. Aware of the snow, the plant continues to throw up shoots.

When I was a college chaplain I knew a young man who lacked a hand and a good part of his forearm. He was playing baseball for his high school team one day when a stranger showed up at the sidelines, stood around for a while, and then approached him after practice. "Hey, kid," the man said, "you've only got one hand." "Right," replied my young friend, he'd noticed that. "Jeez," the man shook his head, "I'm a scout for [a major league team]. They sent me out to look at you. Nobody noticed you only had one hand." It was a pretty rough sort of conversation, but it underlines how magnificently many young people can adjust to a hard reality with proper support and encouragement.

Kids are tough when they don't have to stand alone. They have the means to endure and to prevail. We tip our hat to this young man's parents, or whoever it was who tossed him a baseball over and over until he figured out a way to catch and throw with one hand, and to bat too. They led him through disability to victory. He had to do it himself but not without the presence of a hopeful older person. The gardener mulches, but then knows to clear away the mulch to allow the shoots to harden off in the cold and make their move. Different plants need different kinds of care. Difference is important, but the future is there for all things.

Does this include us? Do we live in a way consistent with our grandchildren, our garden? What can we learn from the young? What can we learn from the natural world in which we live?

The issue really isn't the "What," the content of learning, as much as it is whether we are open, available to learning. What will keep us healthy as aging people, spiritually healthy as we stand before the God who in the Bible is always moving her people into the future, is our stance vis-à-vis God's presence with us as we move ahead.

I don't mean that the world necessarily moves *forward*, in the sense of improving, getting better, progressing. We all know, from the history of the twentieth century, that the notion of inevitable progress has been mortally battered; that, for example, new discoveries in science, while providing enormous benefits (nuclear medicine) have also provided horrendous opportunities for destruction (nuclear weapons). But the world does *change*; it's a complicated place. And, in some peculiar way, our task as the young-old is to grapple with that world, understand it, and use our experience of history and the past, our wisdom, our "concern with life itself in the face of death itself" to lead those who are younger into thoughtful approaches to the

changing world. In short, we can't use what we pecu-
liarly have, our hard-worn reflective wisdom, if we
aren't aware and understanding of the world to which
it must be applied. The young, all the young who surround us, are in a way our children now. And it is
from parenting that we get our best clues on how to
handle living in this new world.

If parents are healthily identified with, though
thoughtfully separate from, their children's well-being,
the inevitable failures and heartbreaks hit them hard:
misbehavior, lack of success in school, difficulty in
making friends, trouble at work, perhaps losing a lover
or partner. I remember talking to a student who had
seriously misbehaved and had been dismissed from
school. "The worst is the quiet in the house and seeing my father sitting in the bedroom by himself looking out the window." We all probably know what it is
like to have been disappointed by someone we care for
and trust.

Even the most supportive, loving parents are sometimes struck a little dumb by the things their progeny
do and take a while to get over it. But parents do get
over it and remain hopeful and encouraging while
maintaining moral lines of strength. Almost every
high school teacher knows parents who are more
struck down than their kids when college hopes are
not borne out in the admissions process. Given a day
or two to kick the walls and swear, the kids are usually busily planning their life at the college they got in
to. When the parents come to comfort the child, they
find someone busily about the future; the parents are

still stuck in the rejection and the hurt they assume their child feels.

Those of us who are known by the God of the future, people who have experience in the world, are connoisseurs of development. We look to the end, to the possibilities, only to the best, to the vision and, if we are doing our job, we are whispering in the ear of our college-bound young friend, who perhaps lives next door, "that's a perfectly good place to which you're going and you're going to be terrific there. And, by the way, if you don't like it there, get all As and transfer." In short, in the midst of winter, if we have aligned ourselves with God, we see the buds and shoots of spring, and we know that, sooner or later, they will blossom.

While some parents may be shaking their heads and wondering where this is all going to end, the rest of us, the connoisseurs of development, are standing firm. Some parents may be saying buckle down and walk this straight and narrow path and you'll end up with the corner office and won't we be proud; but a wise adult is saying, perhaps somewhat subversively, maybe you should take a year off and ski, or travel around the world; you can stay at youth hostels, it won't cost that much, there's a little school in Australia where maybe you can teach—I'll help you find out about that. Can you imagine that we, the establishment as it were, the guardians of the past, are also subversive in the present?

We might well lead a young person to question the slippery slide to commercial success and wonder if a happier and more fulfilled life might be in being of service to people no matter in what profession. In relation to young people we say: "You can be more of a person, a deeper person, you can see through the peripheral and trivial, and have the strength to look into the depth of things. You are strong and young and beautiful, fly!"

But that is possible only if those of us who know those young people have looked over our lives in a serious way and found the solid ground out of which such a presence can speak.

One of my young friends for years sought to prove himself in various sports, but he actually was not much of a hand-eye coordination fellow. He always ended up on the JV, and fairly low down. What he could do was run, but hardly anyone in the family had done that. Toward the end of his high school career he decided to try it and did well. He clearly had potential. When he went to college on the West Coast, he went out for cross-country but was intimidated by some of the near world-class runners and by the two-a-day practice schedule which he was sure would interfere with his academic work. However, he continued to run on his own and to get advice from one of his old coaches. He got stronger as he got older; his times gradually improved. He ran in several challenging races, did well, and built up a kind of resume of good racing times.

One day this young man realized he was running as well as many people on the college team, so he gulped, took a chance on being rejected, and asked for an appointment with the coach. Impressed with the times (in my experience, running coaches can be skeptical of people who walk on, but times are a sure convincer), the coach invited him to come out. The commitment at that level is substantial both in time and energy, the work-outs are draining, and the schedule demanding. His parents were doubtful, what was this strange new world to which their son seemed to be so committed, but his dear nearly one-hundred-year-old grandfather, a man of the future, said gruffly, "You can work on your academics in graduate school!"

The door opened and the young man walked through to more challenge than he could have imagined, but also to a lot of satisfaction. His grandfather, who happened to meet him in the polling station one election and announced to all present, "Damn it, he's come to cancel all my votes!" was gratified, and the bond between them strengthened. Note the perspective from which he saw his grandson, how different it was from the parents, and how it was tied to the grandfather's hope and trust in the future? Better yet, can you imagine how that young man feels about his grandfather, the one who gently pushed him toward a developing future?

The old man could see beyond the present into the future, he could see beyond the daily to the broad sweep of life. In the midst of the decline of his body, he was able to rejoice in the power of his grandson's body. In a wonderful way he could see a powerful possible present reality and was willing to make room, even in his own political commitments, which are strong, for his grandson. Is there any wonder that the old man passed the century mark?

What was the grandfather teaching about what is essential and important in life by his attitudes and direction? What was he saying about what really matters, what is, to use a well-worn phrase, of ultimate concern? When we look to the future we are witnessing to the God of the living, not of the dead. God is Lord of the future; she has swallowed up the past into the future.

Does the past matter? Of course it matters, but in our experience it matters too much. We all know people who live in the past, who deplore everything about the present, who scorn the young, sneer at technology, and who have nothing much good to say about anything. A friend spoke to me once of his mother whom he said was "the Queen of Disapproval." There are people who have the resources to live as if the present never happened; they are happiest in the styles and attitudes of the past, in a world which was often honorable and fine, sometimes not so honorable and fine, but which is still a world of the past.

Perhaps it is easier to live with a God of the dead, not of the living, to deify, that is, to worship or absolutize the past, not to see that things have been broken down and built up, have been destroyed and grown again. It is easy to say that rock and roll, rap, and country music are simple-minded forms of music, not recognizing either that popular music has never been complex or that in the hands of many musicians those contemporary forms reach toward the complexity of jazz, itself an art form thought to be not very respectable not so long ago. Many of us get our opinions from a narrow range of media, forgetting that there's been a change in the stance of media, particularly the news-reporting organizations, from journalism to entertainment. We need to watch and listen for ourselves, if we are to be close to the God who shares life with people. This will help us truly to be the people of God, growing with God into the future.

I know an elderly writer, a man of some reputation amongst those who know good writing. To read his work is to enter a world of clarity, but also to experience prose which is warm and lively. Now old and quite frail, he is also, in his own way, as you might expect from his work, a delightfully frisky man. A short while ago he published a book collecting of some political reporting he'd done over the years. Beautifully written, the essays ring with hope and goodness. To read him is to know him, a man of elegance and hope. Presuming on our acquaintance, I wrote him a note of thanks for the book. His response was a page of elegant gratitude. He chooses to live as a hopeful human in the middle of a political and social atmosphere he deplores. Full of foreboding, he will not give up hope. For him things are always moving on—a glorious summer is on the way, in every way. He lives with the buds and the shoots.

My elderly friend's message is a message about nature and about people, but I would take it that our hope is also in God who brings life out of death. The sprouts and buds of spring are present in February; the sprouts and buds of useful life are present in sloppy teenagers, especially if the mature people around them, living out of their own experience of hope, are known as men and women of hope, people of the living, not of the dead. "Damn it," stamped the old man, "he's canceling all my votes!" And the old man laughed and laughed.

This doesn't mean that every new idea is great and will save the world. How much blood has been shed over the notion that progress is inevitable if everyone will just agree on one ideology or another? There are no easy answers to the difficult questions of economic and political disarrangement, of how community can be built in the middle of social disintegration, how popular culture can build up and serve people rather than be a vehicle for profit-making through violence and misogyny. We have lived through enough styles and fashions to know that styles and fashions are just that. We have at least experienced the wartime forties, the quiet fifties, the wild sixties, the weird seventies, the materialistic eighties, the booming nineties, and the deflating new century. And we know that ideas, styles, and fashions die, but God is not a God of the dead but of the living, and we rise again in God to struggle anew.

For many years the founding headmaster of the school at which I taught (I say many years because he served from 1884-1940, that is to say, *many* years) prohibited the singing in chapel of John Greenleaf Whittier's hymn which begins, "Once to Every Man and Nation" because it contained the line ". . . time makes ancient good uncouth." Dr. Peabody did not think, especially as he grew older, that ancient good could possibly become uncouth—good was good, no matter how old. He might even have thought (as he himself grew older) that the older good was, the more couth it became, as it were. He may have been right about ancient good not being necessarily "uncouth," but time certainly makes ancient good . . . old. It isn't bad because it's old, but it needs examination, just as much as new good needs examination, and, for that matter, just as our grandchildren are examined by the pediatrician and as we ourselves hop (well, crawl) onto our doctor's examining table once a year.

That the new is exciting, intriguing, unfamiliar, perhaps useful, but never without "the vanity and futility of seeking perfection" is important to us. We will realize that while every idea and new contribution may not be valuable, it should be considered, given a break, because, given the state of our civilization, which is probably not that much worse than most civilizations, we need every bit of wisdom and insight we can get. Nothing new is likely to be any more perfect than ideas from the past, and above all, seeking, or expecting, perfection is a vanity and ends in futility.

God is alive, not dead. God is changing and growing in our conception as we are changing and growing, being known by God. Our knowledge of God will always be seeming, that God is, in fact, inexhaustible in her depth, in her riches, and also in her leading us to empty and barren places where we can recover the hope which we need in order to be human. We have all been refreshed by very old people who live so much, so intensely, so much into the future, often with great joy and good humor, like my elderly writer friend.

The good news is that God is present everywhere—in history, in whatever is happening, wherever life is growing out of death, everywhere people stand for justice and freedom, for human dignity and compassion, wherever ideas for bringing separated people together are flowing. And particularly, God is present with people as they grow into themselves, selves which they should not underestimate because they are capable of being so many things.

That God is a God of the living, not of the dead, present not in perfection and surety but in the stumbling, bumbling process of creation, is an idea we live out as we ourselves are open to the future. That God has more hope for us than we ever can imagine is something we have learned through the springing presence of life and hope around us. And if it is a "fond, foolish" hope, then we will perhaps be surprised by joy one day when we turn out to have been right. But we will never become people of hope if we haven't been engaged in the world, grounded in our own hope. The hope we have for the future is a reflection of the hope we have for ourselves, for the universe—a hope which is itself a reflection of the hope God has for us, hope beyond anything we could dream.

In the midst of winter when we had neither hope nor even thoughts about the garden, "there lives the dearest freshness deep down things"; new life was springing up. When we were young and babes-in-arms, the same dearest freshness sprung up in us. We are witnesses, prophets, ones who are sure to offer this hope to God, sure that it is being poured back upon us hope on hope. I have learned that I am called to be, in my old age, still a man of the future, and that it is God who is calling me to join him there.

CONCLUSION

I n this book we've been searching together for the truth of our lives, the truth which God loves. Standing at a penultimate point, we've used our rich experience of life to understand something of the journey, something of the way God's love for our truth has made that truth precious and wonderful. "This is the Lord's doing, and it is marvelous in our eyes" (Psalm 118:23).

On the other hand, perhaps our lives haven't always been marvelous. Some of the choices that were made, perhaps some of the directions that were taken, might be called in retrospect less than wise. Nonetheless, at this point we can usually find something either to appreciate or to learn from what happened to us. There are ways in which in life there is no gain without a loss, no loss without a gain. Jonathan Franzen's celebrated novel *The Corrections* makes this point well. Looking back, his characters see that every good that happened to them involved a loss, and every down involved a gain. Enmeshed as they were in living life, they often could not see the developing pattern. It's the old forest/tree problem.

So it goes with all our lives. Gains and losses are mixed. The trick has been to realize when we are bored, burned out, or have had enough to keep looking for the real stuff of life.

There is the reality of what we have done, or not done, which has been not a mistake, not stupid, not just dumb, but wrong. We deeply regret that there were times when we did not live the truth that was in us, didn't speak up for the right, were not ourselves before God, but also that we acted in ways which were profoundly hurtful to others. Everyone has done those things. It's important for us courageously and honestly to face those issues and regrets.

One of the great modern insights has been that the role of the "tragic hero," once reserved, it was thought, for those in high place (kings, etc.), is a part which is also played by ordinary men and women. We realized, through the genius of Arthur Miller, that Willy Loman, the lead character in *Death of a Salesman*, had a kind of tragic dignity which elicited from his spouse the famous words "Attention must be paid." We might like to think we are better human beings than Willy Loman, but all in all, we recognize in him our brother, even ourselves, who fell from grace because of a flaw of personality. In ancient theater the heroes all suffered from a flaw—most characteristically uncontrolled, and uncontrollable pride and rage—and it leads to suffering for the self and others. However, through the suffering which ensued, there emerged a kind of glory, wisdom, and acceptance of the self—a "terrible beauty," acceptance of self as flawed, and hope for the self in its tragic dignity.

That same terrible beauty and tragic dignity came home to us in the stories of the firefighters who risked and gave their lives when the World Trade Center Towers fell. In *Firehouse,* David Halberstam tells the story of his local firehouse which sent off two rigs to the World Trade Center with thirteen men aboard. One firefighter returned. In telling their story, he does not feel the need to cover up or sentimentalize the men who died. He makes us aware of the courage and moral splendor that shines through the pattern of their lives without ignoring their all-too-human warts and flaws. In giving them the dignity of their flaws, the truth of their lives, he engenders hope in all of us.

It is the gift of modern thinkers that we understand that the tragic hero of the ancient world is present in our life also. We are people who, because of some flaw in our character, acting fully confident of our right and duty to do as we have seen best, acting justly as we in our blindness have seen it, have fallen tragically from the best that we could do and be. We have perhaps taken a good aspect of our personality, our passion, our need for order, our confidence in ourselves, and twisted it into an act which today we truly regret. We have most often let down those closest to us, that which we least intended to do.

In short, we are the tragic heroes of the drama of our lives. We could live refusing to see ourselves clearly, to acknowledge the truth of ourselves; on the other hand, we could live possessed by regret. It would not be right to live owned by the past. We ought not to live either blind or possessed. We need to accept the reality of our falling short of being the person we ought to have been, and in whatever spiritual ways are close to us redeem those moments, leaving them behind as we embrace the reality of our wisdom, which is to accept ourselves as the flawed, fallen people we are before God. This is our victory, our snatching life from life, to live victoriously into the future in full knowledge of our failures, to see ourselves as the battered, broken hero of the drama of our lives. This is the hopeful quality of the life we live in these last great acts of our lives. It is the ground of true humility and the source of our joyful freedom.

Touching real life involves rubbing up against the sloshiness of life as it is lived, paradoxically a key to fullness in every time of our times. If it hasn't seemed possible before, perhaps there is time to do it now. This doesn't necessarily mean shaving our heads, living in a teepee, running twenty miles a day, moving to Burma, wearing only clothing made from hemp, or buying a motorcycle, though it might mean one of those things. I'd stick with acquiring a sporty car myself. One of my friends retired, and a month later drove by a used car lot featuring the little red convertible she'd joked about all her life as her dream car. She didn't pause for a second, simply turned into the lot, looked over the car, traded hers in, and drove away, a happy woman. I think we can be allowed one extravagant gesture to mark this new life.

However, most of the changes I noted are the artifacts of impulse of a kind of superficial heroism. I don't think the world needs more than a few of that kind of hero, most of whom get tired of it pretty soon anyway. Just as one of my students suddenly wondered why, at age twenty-two, he was working a hundred hours a week in an investment bank, superficial heroism wears out quickly. We turn to the true heroism which knows the self as flawed and broken and moves on into the future.

What we need to do, once again, is live fully in whatever stage of life we're in, including the young-old, and retirement. And that does mean touching people where they are as part of our ordinary routine, and exposing ourselves to feel, as the aging and remorseful King Lear said, "what wretches feel." He says, "I have ta'en too little care of this." We might find ourselves, if we have spent our lives in cosseted, symbolically gated, protected social environments, drawn to those who haven't, to do whatever we can to be present to them. And this would be for our sake, not for theirs. When I say live fully in each stage of life, I mean by "fully" not only depth of experience but also breadth of experience and exposure. If we haven't lived with that kind of fullness before, then perhaps the time has come to do so in whatever quiet and simple way God calls us. That might mean driving older people to the doctor, being a classroom aide at a local school, or doing something simple and satisfying in our community—not being a hero or in charge, just being human.

Life is always a challenge; it was when we were young, and it still is. Just as we would not have thought of refusing the challenge in various other stages, our present age is no time to refuse the challenge. Enlightened, emboldened, torn and worn a little by our experience, slightly ironic in our manner, we are not wild enthusiasts; we are the battered survivors of all life could throw at us, and we are invaluable in the world. Give us a minute to recover and we are the insatiable consumers of reality, the new life which springs up around us.

That new life which grows out of our present circumstance is the new springtime which opens to us. We may be of a "certain age," but wherever we walk, life can grow around us, in us, and for others.

JOHN F. SMITH is an educator and retired Episcopal priest, serving for many years as chaplain and teacher at Groton School in Massachusetts. Smith graduated from the University of Michigan and received a master of divinity from the Episcopal Theological School. He has two grown daughters and three grandchildren. *Living Forward* is Smith's third book, following most recently *Raising a Good Kid* (Sorin Books, 2002). Smith is happily retired— and living forward on Cape Cod.